THE TWO
MADONNAS

The Politics of Festival in a
Sardinian Community

Second Edition

SABINA MAGLIOCCO
California State University, Northridge

**WAVELAND
PRESS, INC.**

Long Grove, Illinois

For information about this book, contact:
   Waveland Press, Inc.
   4180 IL Route 83, Suite 101
   Long Grove, IL 60047-9580
   (847) 634-0081
   info@waveland.com
   www.waveland.com

Leabharlann James Hardiman

Ollscoil na hÉireann, Gaillimh

D2000

Copyright © 2006 by Waveland Press, Inc.

ISBN 1-57766-372-1

All rights reserved. No part of this book may be reproduced, stored in a retrieval system, or transmitted in any form or by any means without permission in writing from the publisher.

Printed in the United States of America

7   6   5   4   3   2   1

For Bettina
and for "ET"

Contents

Preface to the Second Edition

I first visited the village I call "Monteruju" in the summer of 1983, shortly before the death of my grandmother. I was twenty-three years old, in my second year of graduate school, and I had gone to Sardinia to see Bettina, the woman who had been my caretaker when I was a child and who had worked for my grandmother as a domestic for nearly thirty years. Bettina had retired to her home village—a town familiar to me from her stories since my earliest childhood. A sense of excitement and adventure permeated the trip for me, from the long ferryboat journey from Civitavecchia, to the hot, dusty train ride across the island, to the creaky, bumpy private taxi that finally delivered me to the village in a cloud of dust. At last, I was going to see this mythical place I had heard so much about; I would not only see Bettina, whom I had not seen in several years, but also her nieces and nephews, her elderly father, and the house in which she grew up, with its dirt floors and hole in the roof for a chimney.

More significantly, I imagined I was going to see real European folklore—the kind I read about in the myriad books and articles I was consuming as part of my graduate training in folkloristics and anthropology. I was not disappointed. In the space of my brief visit, I found women weaving on four-harness looms, cheese being produced in small huts on the mountain, and Tiu Dominigu, the local healer, removing the evil eye. Daily life was punctuated by the sound of bells: the hourly tolling of church bells and the ever-present chiming of sheep bells in the background.

But I could also see that Monteruju was rapidly changing. In 1983 it had electric street lights and running water, television and phones, and most of the people I spoke with continually compared the "traditional" and "modern" paradigms (cf. Saunders, 1981; Herzfeld, 1987), telling me how much things had changed in the last fifteen years. Most of them said things had changed for the better: life was easier; there was no more hunger or *miseria* (wretched poverty); there were many conveniences. Yet I also sensed a growing nostalgia for the old days, especially in conversations about festivals. This condition, which Michael Herzfeld (1987) has called "cultural disemia," intrigued me, perhaps because it mirrored my own conflicted ambivalence between romanticism and materialism. I like to say that Monteruju got into my blood that summer. The day I left Bettina, I looked up at the mountain looming red over the town and I knew, with a certain sense of destiny, that I would be back—that this was the place where I would do my dissertation fieldwork.

It has been over twenty years since I first visited Monteruju, and more than ten since this work was published in English. Looking back now, it is easy to see that I was documenting the process of Monteruju's transition into a global economy, and the resulting effects of globalization on its festivals. In the mid-1980s, globalization studies were in their infancy, and I lacked the theories to explain what I was documenting in broader terms. In this second edition, I am now able to frame *The Two Madonnas* in terms of a more contemporary understanding of globalization and its effects, as well as provide an account of what has happened to Monteruju—and my complex relationship to it—in the last ten years.

✺

The Politics of Globalization

Anyone studying culture within the last fifty years has become aware of a network of processes, difficult to isolate from one another but clearly perceptible, which are changing the nature of cultures and the ways they interact with one another on numerous levels. Scholars have called this process *globalization*. Each discipline has produced its own concept of globalization, but its parameters include the spread of market capitalism and the internationalization of business; the increasing density of international relations and global politics; the mass movements of peoples across national boundaries; the emergence of a "world society" beyond the nation state, transcending old divisions such as urban/rural and center/periphery; cultural homogenization; and the emergence of postcolonial cultures (Appadurai, 1990:296–299).

Globalization is often interpreted as the growing Westernization or Americanization of world cultures; however, this problematic perspective implies a one-way movement of culture "from the West to the rest," ignoring cultural flows that move in many directions. Moreover, a focus exclusively on Americanization ignores the more profound threat, for peripheral areas, of absorption by nearby large-scale polities (Appadurai, 1990:295)—for example, in the case of Sardinia, "Italianization" or "Europeanization" may be in many respects more significant dangers than Americanization. As Arjun Appadurai argues, "The central problem of today's global interactions is the tension between cultural homogenization and cultural heterogenization" (1990:295). One of the central features of globalization is that homogenization and commercialization of cultural phenomena are frequently accompanied by strong oppositional movements for localization in a climate in which identity is construed as difference. This often leads to the reclamation of previously abandoned cultural forms that become symbols of local identity, as was the case of Monteruju and much of Sardinia in the 1980s and 1990s.

This book explores how Monteruju's reaction to these tensions manifested in two of its major festivals: the Assumption of the Blessed Virgin and Santa Maria di Runaghes. During the 1980s, as the Assumption became more oriented towards a tourist market, Monteruvians revived a previously moribund festival in honor of a local madonna, Santa Maria di Runaghes. This revival or "reclamation," as I later came to call it (Magliocco, 2001), was important because festivals serve as performance events that construct and negotiate meanings for both insiders (Monteruvians, in this case) and outsiders (tourists, guests, returning émigrés, visiting anthropologists, and other representatives of the global community). Thus, who controls festivals and what identity is performed become crucial questions. In the process of this transformation, the festivals became politicized as part of the struggle between an incumbent socialist administration with a progressivist agenda firmly rooted in Enlightenment programs, and an emerging center-right coalition that found its voice by trumpeting the values of the rural, the "authentic," and the exquisitely local.

Part of the reason for what became an intense and bitter ideological struggle played out, in part, in festivals was rooted in the economic and global dynamics of Sardinia in the 1980s. Like other rural Sardinian towns, Monteruju stood on the threshold of globalization; the old world of peasant economies and values had not disappeared, but the global economy and consumer capitalism were already at the door. Globalization and its twin, localization, were just emerging as discourses on the public stage. Rather than representing competing discourses of center versus periphery, or of "traditionalist" versus "modernist" paradigms, the development of separate festivals for outsiders and locals, where different and contrasting sets of identities are performed, must be viewed as part of the twin processes of globalization and localization—"not two arguments, two opposing views of what is happening in the world today, but two constituitive trends in global reality" (Friedman, 1990:311). The globalization of the Assumption and the reclamation of Santa Maria, like the conflict between Monteruju's socialist junta and the Christian Democrats, were part of the same process. Instead of interpreting the patronal feast as "folklorized" or "touristicized" and Santa Maria di Runaghes as "genuine" or "traditional," both festivals, as well as the process of festival reclamation itself, must be seen as part of the same phenomenon.

꒦꒦

Monteruju and Its Festivals in the New Millennium

Since the early 1990s, Monteruju has continued on its path into the glo-bal economy. The trends I described in the first edition of this book have con-tinued: there has been a steady increase in the town's links with, and dependence on, the outside world, accompanied by a greater penetration of state and world institutions into the private lives of its citizens. At the same time, interest in the local has increased and has manifested in a multitude of cultural events, from festivals to local art and photography exhibitions to the creation, in November 2000, of the village's own cancellation postage stamp with an image St. Martin, its co-patron saint, spearheaded by the St. Martin festival committee of 2000. In the spring of 2001, the village acquired its own Internet Web site (www.bessude.it\), filled with old photographs of the vil-lage before its transformation in the 1980s and 1990s—once again emphasiz-ing the linkage between a rural peasant past and the creation of a local identity for public consumption.

At the same time, the heated political climate of the late 1980s and early 1990s has abated considerably. After the fall of communism in the winter of 1989–1990, the Italian Left underwent significant reorganization and for a time was unable to present a coherent agenda, allowing right-leaning parties to grab power in a number of national and local races. Monteruju's local elec-tions reflected this trend as well, though with some delay. After reigning essentially undefeated for two mayoral terms, in the late 1990s the Christian Democrat Marta Pinna and her allies faced challenges and discontent from within the Center-Right coalition they had forged. In the spring of 2001, Monteruvians faced another local election, for which Marta's allies were unable to assemble a list of candidates. Instead, the townspeople elected a number of candidates from a collective list representing a number of different families and political viewpoints, headed by one of Marta's former allies who is now a challenger. The town councilors formed a coalition serving a broad range of interests rather than a single political ideology.

In the festive sphere as well, there have been shifts in sides and a soften-ing of attitudes. In an e-mail dated May 1, 2001, my friend Elena Tanca, or "ET," as she prefers to be known to outside audiences, writes:

> In local as well as national politics, traditional alliances have shifted con-
> siderably. On the festival committees, political allegiances are no longer
> as marked or evident [as they were] when you were last here—although
> underneath it all, certain loyalties and differences persist, albeit in an
> attenuated mode. But in festivals, as in politics, there has been a certain
> reshuffling of roles and power in respect to even the recent past.

❦

Postscript

I wish I could say that this information came from recent field trips to Monteruju; but alas, this is not the case. I have not returned to the village since the summer of 1992. In part, this was due to the fallout that ensued after the publication of this book in Italian, a situation I described in the preface to the first edition. In 1989, the local town council, then dominated by the Christian Democrats, had encouraged me to publish an Italian version of my dissertation in a series edited by a colleague at a nearby university. Once they saw the manuscript, however, they felt deeply disappointed by my portrayal of their village, especially my focus on the economic and political forces of globalization and their effects on the community. Although it was not my intent, they felt their village came off looking backwards and poor, and they nixed the book's publication. My Sardinian colleague who had originally expressed interest in publishing the book in his regional academic series lived in a town dominated by the same political party. When he learned of the council's reaction, he also withdrew support. After a time, Monteruju's socialist ex-mayor came to my defense, and in 1995 we found a publisher willing to print the manuscript. But the Christian Democratic majority was so angered by this development that they took their revenge by expropriating lands which belonged to the families of my supporters, ostensibly to build a road up the mountain, but for all intents and purposes depriving them of the meager income they drew from the fruit and olive orchards.

Despite my theoretical knowledge of politics and power in Mediterranean villages, I was deeply troubled by this turn of events. It seemed that my very presence in the village had become a poison to the individuals whom I most loved and to whom I owed the greatest debt. Reluctantly, I decided not to continue my work in Sardinia, at least until the political situation had calmed down and I could return without causing controversy.

This distressing situation coincided with local reactions to the disintegration of my marriage. My status as a "halfie" had always meant that I was held to many of the same behavioral standards as local women, and this extended to what was expected of me after my marriage in 1988. When I returned to the field in 1989 with my then-new husband, he was received very graciously by all my friends in the village. But almost immediately, I began to draw criticism for my "unwifely" behavior—spending long hours away from home conducting interviews, working on the computer instead of cooking and cleaning, and in general not conforming to village expectations of proper behavior for a married woman. "You are behaving exactly as you did with your grandmother, always acting according to your own mind!" Bettina scolded, to which I brazenly retorted, "Who else's mind should I act according to?"

In the summer of 1992, as my marriage was beginning to suffer signs of stress, I decided to stop in Monteruju on my way to Ogliastra, where a graduate student of mine was working on a colleague's group research project. Perhaps I was seeking in my field relationships some of the closeness I was missing at home; or perhaps, as Kirin Narayan once suggested to me, fieldwork offers a kind of escape to anthropologists when our personal lives become too complicated and uncomfortable. During this visit, I was to stay for part of the time with my friend ET and her sister. But possibly because she sensed the unconscious reasons for my visit, ET's sister had strong objections to my very presence. My relationship with her had always been strained; she had long objected to my friendship with her sister, often calling attention to the class differences between us by giving me the nickname *sa fiza de sa pudda bianca* (the daughter of the white hen). She was so offended by my inappropriate behavior as a married woman that she publicly forbade me from returning to their house. In drawing a line of demarcation between my own behavior and what was expected of local women, she called on differences of class rather than of culture or nationality, stating, "The granddaughter of the marchioness is not welcome in my home."

This public chastisement made it very difficult to continue my friendship with ET. Women's friendships depend on the intimacy of the home and kitchen, which is considered women's territory, to flourish, since meeting in bars and public places is not an option. Since I was banned from her house, there was nowhere else we could really meet. As ET owned land jointly with her sister, meeting in their field or orchard did not feel right, either. Besides, we could easily be seen there, and our meetings could be reported back to her sister, leading to negative consequences for ET at home. Worse, while Elena regretted what had happened with her sister, she was not especially sympathetic towards me. In a miserable conversation during which we tried to sort out what had happened to get me banned me from her house, she reproached me: "It would have been better if you hadn't come this summer. You behaved amorally and inhumanly [by leaving your husband alone to return to the field]. Your place is by his side." When my marriage ended in divorce two years later, many of my village friends, including ET, believed I was ultimately at fault for not having fulfilled my wifely obligations.

In the years since then, the love, good will, and patience Bettina and ET bear me have won out, and they have, I hope, forgiven me. ET now has e-mail, and we communicate frequently. I hope someday to return to Monteruju; yet despite the frequent e-mails and phone calls, it now seems to me like a land of lost contentment. Ironically, ET had once predicted this situation. It was May of 1986, and we were standing on the terrace of her house, looking out over the red tile roofs of the town below as swallows reeled in the sky and little green lizards darted in and out of the tiles. "After you've been gone awhile," she said, "Monteruju and everything about it will start to seem very far away to you, like one of the magical worlds you invented for yourself as a child, or like something out of a dream." And the moment she said it I knew it was true; there was nothing else I could say.

Sabina Magliocco
Los Angeles, California
May 2005

Preface to the First Edition

Field research is almost always a kind of reciprocal endeavor, a product of the "chemistry" (for lack of a better term) between ethnographers and the personalities and cultural circumstances they encounter. While this has always been the case, anthropologists have only recently begun to openly acknowledge it,[1] and folklorists, who sometimes operate in a time warp, have been reluctant to follow suit. In this work, I have followed the practice of many folklorists and kept myself, my own feelings and observations, and relationships with my collaborators out of the way of the theory and descriptions that follow. But this does not tell the whole story of my ongoing relationship with the people of Monteruju, my perspective while doing this research, or its politicization within the community following its translation into Italian. These are as much a part of this study as the politics of festival; indeed, they are part of the same process. My intention here is to contextualize my research by situating myself in the field much as I have situated my informants, to explain how I came to this study and how I became a part of it, and ultimately how the study itself came to be entangled in the same web of alliances and allegiances as the festivals.

Lila Abu-Lughod has commented on the particular dilemmas faced by fieldworkers who are women and "halfies" (Abu-Lughod, 1991:137). I share many of the characteristics she delineates, although in this study my focus was not exclusively on gender and I am not properly a halfie. I grew up partly in the United States and partly in Italy, where my family spent summers. My parents had emigrated from Italy during the 1950s, both professionals who were fleeing devastated European economies for greener pastures in the United States. I was familiar with many aspects of bourgeois urban Italian culture, but Italian folk culture, including festivals, was outside my family's cultural scope. My exposure to it came chiefly through Bettina, a Monteruvian woman who worked as a domestic for my grandmother and cared for me during many of those summers. It was because of Bettina's stories that I first became interested in Sardinia and the possibilities of doing research there. Thus, I entered the field squarely in the paradigm of Charles Perrault and the brothers Grimm, seeking in Sardinia the same alternative to bourgeois culture and transgressive escape from its limitations that many nineteenth-century folklorists had sought.[2]

I conducted fieldwork in Monteruju in 1984, 1986, and 1989, for a total period of eighteen months. During my first forays in the field, I lived with Bettina (who had since retired to her hometown) and generally conformed to the role of a daughter studying at the university and living at home. This recognized social role gave me a certain legitimacy within the village. But my role was altogether more complex: while I was Bettina's surrogate daughter, I was also the granddaughter of her former employer. Like Abu-Lughod's halfies, I was and was not "the other." In many ways I was indistinguishable from my peers in the village: I looked like them physically—small, dark, and gracile, as Mediterranean islanders often are; we shared a popular culture, both an Italian one and a globalizing American one, of pop music, films, TV shows, and fashion.

Yet there were also profound differences between us. I came from a privileged background; to many, I represented a system of oppression and dominance, both class and cultural, emanating from "the continent," as Sardinians call mainland Italy. I was also *s'americana*—an appellative by which I am still known in Monteruju—and therefore connected with the United States' cultural and economic hegemony, which is deeply resented in many parts of Europe. Nevertheless, my association with Bettina and her family had many advantages: it provided me with access to the community and instant respectability. Yet it also situated me within a system of alliances and reciprocal relationships which would have many consequences for me in the following years. At first, these were not evident to me, in part because I was unaware of them, and in part because the political strife in Monteruju had not reached the levels it would attain after the municipal elections of 1988.

Outside my "family," my other point of reference in Monteruju was a group of young single women who, like me, were in their early twenties, lived at home, and either attended the university or worked in a nearby city. In this group, I found friendship and emotional support during what was for me an important rite of passage in my life as an ethnologist. When I was not interviewing or doing research, I followed my newfound friends to the café, the public reading room, the pizzeria, and each other's homes, getting to know their families and their way of life intimately. The winter afternoons in front of the fireplace, the early spring olive-picking expeditions, and the seemingly endless summer nights on someone's front step provided excellent occasions for the collection of folkloric data and observations. Because my young friends attended many local festivals, I began to attend with them and became more familiar with their form and structure. My association with this group strongly colored many of my perceptions of festivals, and of Monteru-

vian culture in general. Through them, I became aware of gender and generational conflicts in the organization of festivals. Because some of my friends
were politically active in the local town council, my consciousness of the
expression of political conflict in festivals developed and grew.

Trouble began for me when one friend, whom I call "Elena" or "ET,"
turned out to be from a family with whom Bettina's family had long-standing
disagreements. Bettina began to express disapproval each time I saw her and
tried to prevent me from entering into any kind of relationship with her that
would imply reciprocity between the two families. But I could not stop seeing
her. She was an insightful collaborator, whose position on the town council
and at the head of a festival committee gave me access to valuable inside information. She was also unusually perceptive about her own culture and blessed
with a dry, sardonic wit; a deep friendship had blossomed between us. So I
tried to remain impartial, to retain my friendship with Elena without alienating Bettina and her family. This complicated situation was never resolved; it
continues to be at the crux of my uneasy position in Monteruju today.

In the 1988 municipal elections, the incumbent socialist administration,
in which Elena had served as vice-mayor, was toppled by a Christian Democratic (D.C.) group headed by a woman I call "Marta," who had been in
charge of one of the town's most important festivals just the year before. In
fact, she had spearheaded the effort to restore an antique statue of Santa
Maria and to revitalize the festival. A number of women who had been on
the festival committee with her were also elected to the town council that
year; two of the new councilors were relatives of Bettina and close friends of
mine. The election deeply split the community between supporters of Marta
and the D.C. administration and supporters of the socialist faction, which
was now in the minority. One friend compared the elections to the nuclear
holocaust in the made-for-TV movie *The Day After*. "You'd walk down the
street and everybody was in a state of shock; you hardly knew whom you
could greet and whom you couldn't." The conflict became embodied in a
fierce rivalry between Marta and Elena.

At this point, I felt caught in a dilemma. As fictive kin to Bettina, my loy-
alties should have been to Marta and the D.C., because Bettina's niece and
nephew were allied with her on the town council. But I felt I could not and
should not take sides, both as a professional and because my friendships with
ET and other minority members were meaningful and valuable to me. My
initial goal was to remain as objective as possible, both for the purposes of
research and because within my own worldview, it is not only possible but
correct to remain outside political controversy in order to preserve relations
with all parties involved. This perspective, however, contrasts sharply with
that of many Monteruvians, who consider family loyalty to be the primary
form of political affiliation.

When I returned to Monteruju in 1989 to continue my research, I felt
myself pulled now by one side, now by the other. Marta, Bettina, and my
friends in the D.C. delighted in regaling me with tales of the socialist group's

alleged misdeeds and Elena's confrontational behavior at council meetings. My socialist friends scornfully mocked Marta and her administrative style, and Elena could not restrain herself from pouring out her feelings of bitterness and anger over her political defeat each time we got together. To make matters worse, my exploration of the relationship between festivals and politics only poured salt into the community's already sensitive wound. With each interview I did, I felt disloyal to the opposing faction, and I began to feel that it would be impossible to remain effectively objective.

It was at this point that a professor at a Sardinian university with whom I had had extensive communication approached me with the idea of publishing my dissertation in Italian in a series of which he was editor. He alerted me to the fact that grant money from the region was available for this purpose through each town council; I had only to garner local support and apply for the funds. I was very interested in the idea and rather romantically taken with the notion of giving something back to Bettina and her town, so I approached Marta about it. She supported my idea enthusiastically; we applied for the funds, and I began translating the manuscript.

When my socialist friends got wind of the project, they were furious. They saw it as another way for the D.C. administration to gain fame and glory, and me as a traitor for helping them achieve their ends. To her credit, Elena always supported the project, but as I started working on it our friendship cooled. By the spring of 1990, I had finished the translation and revisions suggested by the series editor. I sent copies of the work to the D.C. majority and asked them to pass it to the opposition when they were through with it. I should specify here that in the Italian manuscript, the issue of the political use of festivals was marginal. However, the work reflected, as does this work, a multiplicity of views and perceptions of festivals; it did not gloss over community conflicts; and it presented, among other things, a discussion of the festival as a vehicle for identity display in which Monteruju often competed with neighboring towns.

These aspects drew heavy criticism from Marta and the majority on the council. Marta felt the work made Monteruju look backwards and unsophisticated. My emphasis on gender and generational conflict in festivals made it obvious to her that I had been influenced by the wrong kind of people who had given me inaccurate information, which turned up in extensive quotations throughout the manuscript. The section which most distressed her was the one in which I discussed Monteruvians in *blason populaire* (popular stereotypes) and folk narrative. While I offered to discuss eventual editorial changes in an open town meeting, she felt so slighted and misrepresented by my work that she decided to withdraw the grant funds we had obtained to finance its publication. Without the partial subvention, the Italian editor refused to publish. He lived in a town dominated by the D.C. and did not wish to risk alienating local party magnates by publishing a work Monteruju's D.C. majority had condemned. So the publication project fell through, and Marta used the funds we had obtained for other purposes.

Clearly, there had been discrepancies in the expectations that each of us had brought to the situation, as well as in our respective perceptions of the goal of the finished product. I expected to write a scholarly work that would interest the community that had generously hosted me. The series editor expected a partial subvention and guaranteed sales of the book to shore up his financially strapped series; he was unprepared for the kind of controversy it generated in the community. Marta perhaps expected an idealized representation of Monteruju, without reference to economic problems, negative stereotypes, and internal conflict which so often draw the attention of continentals writing on "the Sardinian question."[3] She felt hurt and betrayed by my portrayal, as though the guest Monteruju had received so hospitably had suddenly violated the rules of hospitality (cf. Herzfeld, 1987).

Despite my efforts at impartiality, Marta's reaction to my manuscript put me, in the eyes of many people, squarely in the camp of the socialist opposition. Many who had previously opposed publication now interpreted the rejection of the manuscript in a political light: Marta had decided to nix the project because of my friendship with ET. My allegiance to Bettina was apparently overridden by my friendships with members of the opposition party. They became ardent supporters of its publication, although without the majority vote on the town council the project had no chance of ratification. The book became another political football in a game in which virtually any form of cultural production is fair game for political manipulation. In fact, it provided new ammunition for the strife that continues to divide Monteruju.

My experience illuminates the fact that folklorists are now at a historical juncture in which the people they represent are perfectly capable of representing themselves. The ways in which we choose to represent them may in fact be at odds with the ways in which they wish to see themselves, and the two points of view are not always reconcilable. My own responsibility remains to describe and analyze the data I collected; but naturally, they are colored by my experiences and perceptions. In that sense, Marta's criticisms are not unfounded. Because I am sensitive to her concerns, and wish to shield Monteruju and its townspeople from potential embarrassment and further conflict, I have chosen to use pseudonyms for the village and all living informants. While I realize that anyone familiar with northwest Sardinia will probably be able to identify the town, and certainly Monteruvians reading this will recognize themselves, it is a choice that will at least afford them a measure of privacy against an outside world which can be intrusive. I hope it will also spare them any further embarrassment at the exposure of some of the inner workings of their society.

No ethnographic work can convey the whole extent of any cultural experience, and this one is no exception; I apologize to all who feel I have not successfully represented their reality. All errors and omissions are my own.

Sabina Magliocco
Madison, Wisconsin
June 1992

Acknowledgements

Any task of this magnitude would have been impossible to complete without the assistance, advice, and support of many individuals, to whom I owe a tremendous debt. My primary thanks go to the people of Monteruju, without whom none of this would have been possible. Space does not permit me to list them all individually, but special thanks are due to Elisabetta Carta and her entire family; Gavino Cabras and Lorenza Carta; Giuliano Cabras and Edna Murphy; Domenica and Vincenza Carboni; Pinuccia Chessa; Franca Falchi; Giovanni, Minnia, and Tonino Fancellu; Pinuccia and Caterina Laconi; and Chiara Maria Vargiu. Many others have helped me in ways they and I know only too well; because of their hospitality, cooperation, and affection, this is truly a collaborative project.

A number of Italian scholars proved invaluable resources. Carla Bianco, Matilde Callari Galli, Enrica Delitala, Alessandro Falassi, and Maria Margherita Satta each gave of their time and expertise, from which I benefited immensely. In the United States, many friends offered their valuable comments and criticism. My gratitude goes to Regina Bendix, Linda Dégh, Michael Herzfeld, Kirin Narayan, and Edgar Slotkin.

To my family, both in the United States and in Italy, I am grateful for continued support and assistance. Special thanks go to Camillo Callari; Fiora Magliocco Callari; and Barbara, Laura, and Claudia for their extended hospitality and warmth during the times I was in Rome; to Paolo Coretti for sharing with me his unpublished dissertation on Marian cults; and to my parents, E. Bruno Magliocco and Maria Teresa Manente Magliocco. To my husband Uli Schamiloglu I owe perhaps the greatest debt of all, for living the fieldwork and the writing of this book with me both *de facto* and in spirit, and for providing assistance with setting the final copy.

The research for this project was made possible by two grants from the Fulbright Commission.

Notes

[1] The critique of anthropology has developed into a body of literature too vast to effectively review here. For some of the most salient works on reflexive ethnography, see Clifford (1988), Fischer and Fischer (1986), Rosaldo (1989), and Ruby (1982). Folklorists who have made use of a more reflexive approach include Narayan (1989) and Lawless (1981).

[2] Stallybrass and White (1986) have examined the figure of the housekeeper or maid in nineteenth-century bourgeois Europe and the role she played as "other" in the construction of a romantic paradigm involving the transgression of bourgeois boundaries and sensibilities (see especially pp. 149–170).

[3] The objectification of the Sardinian question by the Italian dominant culture is critiqued and contextualized by Pira (1978).

Chapter 1

Festivals,
Social Transformation,
and Conflict

This is a study of the effects of social transformation and conflict on two festivals in Monteruju, a town in northwest Sardinia. Both are religious festivals with an important place in the Roman Catholic liturgical year and historical roots in the religious practices of the Roman and pre-Roman peoples who inhabited the island of Sardinia. The Feast of the Assumption of the Blessed Virgin is celebrated on August 15, and the Feast of the Nativity of the Virgin on September 8. These festivals are two of the most widely celebrated on the island, as well as in the rest of Italy and the Catholic Mediterranean. However, in Monteruju, as in most other Sardinian communities that celebrate them, these festivals have acquired a local flavor and texture that make them unique to that particular community. The two Madonnas are thought of in the popular imagination as having distinct personalities and attributes, and the two festivals differ substantially in history, form, and meaning. The distinctly local nature of these celebrations, combined with the great diffusion of the festivals within Sardinia, make them ideal subjects for an investigation of the effects of social transformation on traditional festivals, and the performance of local issues within the festival context. These are the issues that I call the politics of festival.

Over the course of the last century, Sardinia, an island region off the eastern coast of Italy, has undergone vast changes, primarily as a result of industrialization and urbanization. These changes, common to much of southern Italy, are linked to the Italian economic, cultural, and political situation. The impact of these changes on Sardinia's traditional economy and way of life, language, and cultural distinctiveness has been considerable. As a result, many genres of folklore that were tied to the traditional lifestyle are no longer practiced. Paradoxically, however, festivals have managed not only to survive the onslaught of social transformation, but also to thrive in the new climate. As Gallini (1971:12) noted, "in these last years the [festival] has been the object of very showy forms of revival. . . .The festa is triumphantly entering into the consumer economy." And Manning (1983:4) has gone so far as to state that "throughout both industrialized and developing nations, new celebrations are being created and older ones revived on a scale . . . unmatched in human history."

The entry of festivals into the consumer economy has brought about a number of resulting changes in festival structure, in the function and meaning of festival, and in the structure of the year cycle itself. The same qualities that have enabled festivals to become consumer products also make them vehicles for the playing out of conflicts—both local conflicts and the larger, intrinsic conflicts implied by the entire post-peasant way of life. In Sardinia festivals stand squarely in both worlds: the macro-world of the consumer economy and the micro-world of local concerns; the pre-industrial, agro-pastoral world and the postindustrial one. Like those who organize them and attend them, festivals have a foot in both camps. This basic conflict or contradiction plays out in various ways in each festival, as the organizers grapple with the cultural materials available to them to make a statement through the festival.

☙❧

Festivals and Economic Transformation

Festivals are intimately tied to a community's economy and therefore to its social structure. In many cases, festivals actually celebrate the economy of a town or region through the use of ceremonies and objects symbolically linked to economic practices (Abrahams, 1982:161). In Monteruju, for example, the agrarian and pastoral branches of the local economy, as well as the larger consumer economy and the conflicts among these three systems, all find expression in two important festivals.

Folklorists and anthropologists have only recently begun to express interest in the problem of the interrelationship of economic transformation and festive change. Previously, scholars in the United States especially have tended to focus on a single performance of a festival or ritual in a given time frame in order to fully explore its meaning and function in society as a whole. While there is nothing wrong with this approach, it presumes that cultures are static and unchanging, that one performance of a festival or year-cycle rite is much the same as any other. In fact, nothing could be further from the truth.

The publication in English of the work of Mikhail Bakhtin in 1968 drew attention to the relationship between socioeconomic change and festive expression. Bakhtin was interested in the effects of social change on festival, but in an historic context. He postulated a prehistoric time in which the tragic and comic aspects were united in festival (1968:10). In medieval times, the Catholic Church attempted to extract the comic from the festive in order to forge a stronger link between festivals and the liturgy. But the comic and the tragic continued to exist in juxtaposition in the folk festival. With the rise of the bourgeoisie during and after the Renaissance, however, the nature of folk humor changed again, further severing the comic from the tragic and ending the fecund symbolic inversions of the carnivalesque world. In Bakhtin's view, the symbolic inversions that characterized the medieval festival (and folk humor in general) can exist only within a rigidly hierarchical social structure (1968:17–57ff).

Recently, a number of scholars have noted marked change in festive organization in societies moving from pre-market economies to a consumer economy. Both Waldemar Smith (1977) and Stanley Brandes (1988), working in Latin America, noted that the traditional system of festival financing and organization in areas of Catholic domination undergoes radical change with the shift to a consumer economy. In Sardinia, Clara Gallini and Giulio Angioni have commented extensively on the effects of the consumer economy on the traditional festive system.[1] According to Angioni, the influence of consumerism removes the festival from the control of the townspeople and places it in the hands of technicians belonging to the hegemonic culture outside the village (Angioni, 1973:277). He contrasts this development to what he sees as the previously autonomous nature of festivals as forms of popular expression; like many Gramscian ethnologists,[2] he sees folkloric expressions as offering alternatives to the culture of the dominant classes. Gallini, in an extensive study of Sardinian pilgrimage-festivals, notes that the festival's ludic nature makes it susceptible to the consumer economy, with its emphasis on enjoyment for its own sake on an everyday basis. The commodification of the festa goes hand in hand with its "touristicization," complicated by strong elements of regional consciousness and desires for political and cultural autonomy (Gallini, 1971:13–14). Like Mesnil (1987), Gallini notes that the commodification of the festival has removed most folkloric phenomena from the participatory sphere, turning them into spectator events (Gallini, 1971:15). She ends her introduction to the problem by saying: "If I were to begin another [research project], I believe the central point . . . [would be] an analysis of those contradictions which I am giving here as a priori considerations rather than as demonstrated fact"—the contradictions between the traditional system and the commodified, touristic one, both of which converge in the festival (Gallini, 1971:17).

Unfortunately, Gallini's and Angioni's calls for research have gone largely unheeded; other contemporary scholars of Sardinian folklore have chosen to deal with festivals from a mostly historical perspective. This study is in part an attempt to answer the calls of Angioni and Gallini for more research into the problem of festivals and socioeconomic change. Oddly, neither Italian nor Sardinian ethnographers have concerned themselves with

documenting the effects of social, economic, and cultural change on one festival, and to date Gallini is the only scholar who has tackled the issues of
folklorismus[3] and tourism in festival. The phenomenon, as Gallini indicates
above, is widespread, but current Italian theorists are still intent on the problems of festivals in peasant society. The old peasant model of festival as com-
pensation for exploitation or rebellion against the dominant hegemony does
not explain the folklorization of festival, its transformation into a display of
local identity, or the revival of traditional forms to satisfy modern needs.

Festivals and Social Conflict

Early scholars of ritual and festival, following the Durkheimian model,
tended to focus on the festival's unifying role within the community and to
view it as a "safety valve" for the expression and control of social conflict
within a ludic frame (Gluckman, 1963; Glassie, 1975:126; Turner, 1969).
This model has also tended to dominate Italian studies of festival, where
scholars have examined the unifying role of the festival in the social order
(Gallini, 1971; Pinna, 1971; Lanternari, 1981; Satta, 1982b). According to
these scholars, the festival achieved a temporary atmosphere of unity, or communitas, through a complex system of ritual exchange, as well as through a
number of affective experiences (Smith, 1975) that fostered a suspension of
everyday experience.

But other studies have shown that festivals often serve as catalysts for the
emergence of conflict as well. In Italy, festivals such as the Palio of Siena
(Dundes and Falassi, 1975) and the race of the Ceri in Gubbio (Del Ninno,
1983) have traditionally served to publicly dramatize social conflicts within
the community by formally pitting members of different neighborhoods or
social classes against each other in races, games, and other activities. Yet even
when such conflicts are not normally enacted as part and parcel of the festival
structure, festivals serve as points for the emergence of conflicts intrinsic to the
community. In *The Three Bells of Civilization* (1975), for instance, Sydel Silverman noted the conflicts between the Catholic clergy and the local elite, as well
as between the Church and the Communist Party, as they were played out in
festivals. Silverman showed how the elite of Montecastello, a community in
central Italy, strove to control local festivals as expressions of their own power,
while the clergy acted at times to challenge that power and at others to consol-
idate it (Silverman 1975:166–67). At the same time, the local chapter of the
Communist Party organized political manifestations to conflict with days of
religious festivity and draw participants into its sphere of influence (Silverman
1975:174–76). Thus, we can expect festivals to embody—and even dramatize,
in some cases—existing social and political conflicts in the community.

Major changes in social or economic structure can be expected to
directly affect folkloric expression as manifested in festivals, not only in terms

of the festival's organization and financing, but in its symbolic components as well. Because festivals symbolically display and enact a society's values, they may serve as an accurate barometer of the way in which a community perceives itself and the way it wishes to present itself to outsiders. The kinds of conflicts that emerge during a festival often have important and far-reaching consequences in the social and political life of the community beyond the frame of the festival.

Not all festivals enact or display conflict; in fact, an unwritten rule of many festivals is the suspension of conflicts that ordinarily exist within the community, be they between individuals, families, political parties, genders, or other groups. Nevertheless, whether in the organizational stage or at the level of festive performance, community conflicts usually emerge. It is difficult to predict or to generalize which will predominate at any given time, because so much of the relationship between conflict and festival depends on factors that are exquisitely local and basically unrepeatable. Thus, while one year a theme of political conflict and rivalry may dominate one festival, the following year the community might feel politically united, and some other conflict might be played out. Since in any given community there are usually a number of different conflicts existing at a time (social, economic, political, etc.), it is likely that all of these will be in some way reflected in the repertoire of the community's year-cycle customs.

When discussing conflicts in festivals, it is important to remember that conflict is intrinsic to society; there is no conflict-free community in which conflict-free festivals exist. Festivals, being public rituals on a large scale organized by local individuals with differing backgrounds, economic positions, political opinions, and so on, are bound to be influenced by both individual conflicts and conflicts which characterize the community as a whole. One must also bear in mind that change is intrinsic to the nature of folklore. Variation itself is sometimes used as a criterion for determining the folkloric nature of a given performance or artifact. Festivals, being folkloric productions, are no exception to this rule; no festival is repeated in exactly the same pattern year in, year out, nor has this ever been the case in any historic time. The traditional festival allows variation within a given framework into which innovations must be made to fit; not every change and innovation is necessarily a product of conflict.

Display and Ostentation

Why do so many conflicts seem to emerge around festivals? One reason is that festivals publicly display a community's economy, identity, and values. Yet different community members may have quite different concepts of their town's identity, values, and economic profile. This may lead to a struggle to determine whose values, whose identity will be displayed.

Important in understanding the issues of display and ostentation is a knowledge of the audience which is the intended recipient of the performance, as well as micro-factors influencing the organization of the festival by the "performers" (Hymes, 1975). Traditionally, festivals in Sardinia were put on by community members for community members, plus pilgrims or visitors from nearby towns. Since transportation was difficult and time consuming, few traveled extensively throughout the island just for the purpose of attending religious festivals. Those who did usually had a specific reason, for instance a promise made to a saint to attend his or her festival, or perhaps relatives in a nearby community. These pilgrims and visitors came from communities similar to the ones they visited; while the micro-culture can differ significantly from town to town, these differences were not of the kind to cause great discrepancies in the expectations, tastes, and values of the townspeople versus the visitors.

Thus, festivals in Sardinia traditionally displayed uniquely local concerns: the influence and power of the towns' wealthiest citizens, who usually sponsored the festival; their devotion to the local saint; and the community's economic products and local variants of folk dance, music, and costume. The festival, in fact, was one of the few occasions available for the lavish ostentation and consumption of agro-pastoral products which formed the basis of the community's economy; competitive displays existed between townspeople and among neighboring communities (Lanternari, 1981:132).

The advent of mass tourism has changed this equation by altering the potential audience of each local festival to include individuals from all over the island, from continental Italy, and from the larger world community. With the growth of mass tourism, Sardinia has developed from a relatively isolated Italian province into a mecca for summer tourists seeking a seaside vacation. For many, Sardinia also symbolizes a return to an idyllic, pre-industrial past, replete with picturesque archeological ruins and pre-Christian customs. Italian attitudes towards Sardinia may be characterized by two general views: the romantic one, which finds in every aspect of the culture relics of an ancient and mysterious past, or the denigrating one, which condemns Sardinians as ignorant shepherds engaging in such barbarous customs as blood feuds and livestock theft (Cirese, 1963:82).

In fact, these contrasting views are not as different as they might initially seem: both are products of romanticism and its underlying assumption of cultural evolution, in which peasant society is perceived as closer to a hypothetical primitive past. In the former case, this past is idealized and associated with magic and mystery, while in the latter it is simply dismissed as barbaric, usually on technological and moral grounds. The marketers of mass tourism have capitalized on this mainland stereotype, and brochures advertising Sardinia as a holiday spot often tout the magic and mystery of the many local festivals available for the tourist to experience and enjoy. This marketing ploy has been adopted by Sardinians as well, and every large festival is touted by its promoters as the "most ancient," "most genuine," or "most authentic" event on the island.[4] As a result, previously esoteric traditions with specific roles in the local economy and ritual cycle have in some cases become vehicles for the display of regional identity on a much grander scale.

Like other regional minorities in Europe (McDonald, 1989), Sardinians feel themselves to be distinct from the dominant national culture. Yet they daily confront a situation in which they must conform to a national culture and speak a national language, which pervades their worlds of work, education, government, and entertainment, and which marginalizes them through negative stereotyping and not-so-subtle discrimination. In order to fit in, some believe they must give up their traditional way of life and strong regional identity. But with the mass marketing of local festivals, Sardinians are in fact being asked to publicly celebrate and display the very traits once held up by the dominant Italian culture as examples of their backwardness and isolation. Understandably, in some communities this creates feelings of resentment against tourists and undercuts local enthusiasm for festivals. In some cases, it may even result in the abandonment of the tradition by the locals (cf. Greenwood, 1977).

Take, for example, the case of the *Sagra del Redentore* (Feast of the Redeemer) in Nuoro. Once an occasion for religious devotion and pilgrimage to a shrine overlooking the city, this festival has now become a tourist attraction that brings thousands of spectators to Nuoro from all parts of the island as well as from the continent. A 1986 article in *La Nuova Sardegna* (August 25, 1986, p. 8), the island's largest newspaper, proclaimed: "Among the many spectators, the only ones missing are the Nuoresi." The article continues, in part:

> . . . the August feast has now become almost exclusively a good opportunity to attract thousands of tourists. So much so that the folk groups from different towns are now beginning to desert the traditional parade. Many Nuoresi do not hide their bitterness over the fate of their festival. . . . The majority in fact prefer to temporarily abandon the city, or lock themselves in the house until the end of the hoopla.

A similar situation exists in Monteruju on the occasion of the Feast of the Assumption, although not to such a great extent as in large tourist centers. Many young Monteruvians prefer to go to the beach on the days of the festival, leaving the crowded town altogether, while many older townspeople barricade themselves in their homes against the deafening noise of the rock bands that play in the town square at night. Monteruvians say about these nights: *"Oe este sa festa de sos forestieri"* (Today is the festa for outsiders).

While mass tourism has not yet reached Monteruju, increased mobility between villages has made every festival into a tourist event for spectators from nearby towns. The return of émigrés and the phenomenon of international travel have also influenced the composition of festival audiences. In 1989, for example, one Monteruvian pointed out that five returning émigrés from Australia with their children, an émigré from Switzerland and his Swiss wife, émigrés from Argentina and Germany, plus an American ethnologist (myself) and her Tatar-American husband had been present at the Festival of the Assumption. "Monteruju is becoming an international community," she quipped with a mixture of irony and glee. The demands of a broader, more sophisticated and diverse audience have affected the types of activities and performances likely to wind up on a festival agenda. The wish to look good in the eyes of outsiders, to put on a good show (*fare bella figura* in Italian) may be foremost in the minds of festival organizers. Thus, items of mass culture such as sports events, rock bands, and films may begin to fill the days of the festival.

In addition, music, dance, oral improvisational poetry, and other forms intrinsic to Sardinian festival which were once participatory events have now become staged shows for the benefit of outsiders. These are not put on by townspeople themselves but instead are purchased in the form of paid professional folk music and dance groups who perform on stage for an assembled audience. The performers themselves are usually teenagers who belong to *gruppi folkloristici* (folk dance groups), through which they learned the tradition they are performing.

It is undeniable that changing norms, the influence of the mass media, and tourism have had an impact on festivals in Sardinia. The traditional festival, rooted in an agrarian economy and dependent on the peasant social system, exhibits certain changes when the economy and society that once sustained it have been dramatically altered. Belgian anthropologist Marianne Mesnil has attempted to explain the changes in perception of time and place in what she terms the "folklorized" festival (Mesnil, 1987). Mesnil uses this term to designate a festival that differs from the traditional festival in a number of important respects. According to Mesnil, phenomena such as oral poetry, dance, and music, which are an integral part of traditional festival, appear at the fringes of the folklorized festival as aesthetic products for entertainment or consumption. The festival's focus shifts from the sacred to the aesthetic; the individual performance of music and dance replaces collective participation. The emphasis is on individual consumption of the festival as a product rather than on collective participation and creation of festive productions. "The festival . . . is desemanticized, preserving only certain formal aspects of the original model; it conveys the symbolism of a world vision which has lost its relevance" (Mesnil, 1987:192).

There are many parallels between the "folklorized" festival and the commodification of festivals in Sardinia for the tourist industry, and it is tempting to see in many Sardinian festivals today the desemanticization to which Mesnil refers. However, people do not continue to practice folklore that is meaningless to them. Rather, new elements are combined with older ones to create a form that retains traditional meaning for its practitioners but still reflects and performs their current concerns. Recent years have seen a backlash against the commodification of festivals in certain towns, and the emergence of new motifs within the festive form that play on such ideas as neighborhood solidarity and respect for the natural environment. In 1989, for instance, public displays of historic neighborhood photographs and nature hikes emerged in conjunction with several festivals, including Monteruju's Feast of the

Assumption. At the same time, towns may choose to keep some festivals small and private, for community members only, deliberately resisting the consumer model. Such is the case of Monteruju's Santa Maria di Runaghes.

In this discussion, it is important to bear in mind that traditions change as a result of individual actions. Much as the individual narrator has a large impact on the shaping of his material, individual agents in a given society, acting singly or together, can initiate and introduce changes in the festive tradition which later become traditional themselves. This kind of emergent tradition is usually difficult to trace, but in the case of Monteruju, the recently revived festival of Santa Maria di Runaghes provides a clear example of the impact of individuals on a festival. The revival of this festival in 1979 provided a forum for the introduction of elements which had not been a part of this festival previously, and because the revival is so recent, it is relatively easy to reconstruct the process by which the innovations were introduced.

"Deep Play" and Symbolic Inversion

The concepts of "deep play" (Geertz, 1973a:412–453) and symbolic inversion are important to understanding the meaning of conflicts as expressed within festival. Symbolic inversion is the temporary reversal of everyday norms of behavior that is common to festival (Babcock, 1978:13–38; Davis, 1978; Gluckman, 1963; Turner, 1969; Counihan, 1985; Stoeltje, 1989). It may involve activities such as masking and costuming, parades, licentious or ribald behavior, excessive drinking and feasting, and the like. The 1968 translation of Mikhail Bakhtin's *Rabelais and His World* brought new attention to these carnivalesque and grotesque aspects of some festivals. According to Bakhtin, they formed an integral part of the medieval and Renaissance view of Carnival, which inverted, through humor and symbolic action, the formal, hierarchical world of the medieval European Christian world (1968:5). Each Christian feast had its carnivalesque aspects, which existed as an alternate reality, constrained in space and time by the festival itself, and within which the normal hierarchical order was suspended. The carnivalesque festival world created an alternative to the rigidly structured, hierarchical world dominated by the feudal elite and the Catholic Church. These potentially political aspects of symbolic inversion can make festivals an important forum for the enactment of conflicts and the airing of political dissatisfactions.

It is because festival is usually marked as social play that these otherwise disruptive elements can come to the forefront during festival time. Scholars have called festival time "liminoid" (Turner, 1969) or "time out of time" (Falassi, 1987) because of its qualitative differences from everyday time. Yet the kind of play characteristic of festival is not idle or meaningless, but rather laden with symbolic meaning and significance—what Geertz has called "deep play." Historian Johan Huizinga (1950) developed the concept of symbolic inversion as a kind of adult play. Huizinga theorized that through play, individuals are able to experiment with new roles and ideas; he saw in play a source of renewed energy and creativity in culture, and a forum for the expression of threatening ideas in a nonthreatening environment.

Through festive play, individuals can make important statements about their own communities, statements that sometimes have repercussions after festival time has elapsed. Festive play allows people to experiment with the components of their culture and try out new patterns. Carole Counihan, for instance, has shown how Carnival masking and play in Bosa, Sardinia, allows Bosans to play with the concepts of gender and sexuality as they exist in Sardinian society (Counihan, 1985). And historian Natalie Davis (1978) has demonstrated how images of "women on top" in French Carnival pre-dated social and legal changes in the status of French women. In Monteruju, we will see how the successful organization of a festival by one group of women resulted in their political victory in the following elections.

Not all festivals embody symbolic inversion to the same degree; for example, neither the Feast of the Assumption nor Santa Maria di Runaghes in Monteruju are carnivalesque festivals in the strictly Bakhtinian sense. Yet all festivals involve some suspension of everyday rules of behavior and reversal of daily norms. In many festivals, this often takes the form of licentious behavior, behavior which exists in contraposition to normal, everyday behavioral codes and to the highly proscribed ritual behavior which is often also a part of festival. Excessive drinking and ribaldry are two examples of licentious behavior often found in the festival context.

While it is tempting to see licentious behavior as a kind of "safety valve" which allows pent-up pressures built up during the rest of the year to be explosively released, in practice this is not always the case. In "Christmas and Carnival on St. Vincent" (1972:289), Roger Abrahams rejects Gluckman's "safety-valve" theory of licentious, rebellious behavior as ultimately functioning to uphold the social order. Instead, he proposes that festival portrays "polarities of conflicting attitudes" about behaviors and values in a society. He expands this theory in a later article with Richard Bauman (Abrahams and Bauman, 1978:195), in which he points out that while festival is commonly seen as a reversal of everyday order, the elements of licentiousness and disorder present in festival are in fact present year-round in the society. Moreover, the very same individuals who are likely to violate order in the everyday context are those who will violate it in the festival context, as well. Festival, therefore, cannot be seen as an occasion that reverses everyday norms of behavior, but rather as an occasion in which the ideal norms are openly violated without fear of retribution. In fact, opposing elements in a society— order/disorder, nature/culture, and so on—are drawn more closely together in festival than at any other time of year. This drawing together of opposites actually helps delineate the boundaries between them in a palpable way.

Festival, then, can be seen as a form of symbolic action that temporarily reverses some cultural norms and patterns in order to bring about a greater awareness of these norms, whether by ultimately upholding them or by suggesting alternative modes of behavior. Like all forms of deep play, festivals are profoundly affected by the context in which they take place; factors such as social conflicts and socioeconomic transformation can be expected to have a significant impact on their form and development.

Notes

[1] Because of their spectacular nature, traditional festivals and year-cycle customs in Sardinia have long been objects of study. Early descriptions of festivals can be found eighteenth- and nineteenth-century travel literature, e.g., J. Fuos's *Nachrichten aus Sardinien von der gegenwärtigen Verfassung dieser Insel* (1780), Abbot Francesco Cetti's *Storia Naturale della Sardegna* (1774–1777), Alberto LaMarmora's *Voyage en Sardaigne* (1826), Sir William Henry Smyth's *A Sketch of the Present State of the Island of Sardinia* (1828), and B. Luciano's *Gli Usi e Costumi della Sardegna* (1841). Antonio Bresciani, in *Dei Costumi dell'Isola di Sardegna Comparati con gli Antichisimi Popoli* (1850), attempted to link calendrical practices to rites mentioned in the Bible and Homeric texts. V. Angius's contributions to G.Casalis's *Dizionario Geografico, Storico, Statistico e Commerciale degli Stati del Re di Sardegna* (1833–56) furnish the most extensive description of traditional life in Sardinia in the early 1800s, including many local patronal festivals and calendar customs. For a history of the study of folklore, including festivals, in Sardinia, see Alziator (1978).

[2] Antonio Gramsci has been a major influence on Italian folkloristics. For an overview of his contributions to Italian folklore and ethnology, see Byrne (1982). The Marxist underpinnings of Italian folkloristics are explained in Cirese (1974–75/1); this entire journal issue is devoted to Italian folklore theory. For an overview of Italian ethnography in general, see Saunders (1984).

[3] Folklorismus usually refers to folklore created or altered for the tourist market. For an overview of the development of this concept in Germany and Eastern Europe, see Bendix (1988).

[4] The issue of the authenticity or lack thereof of any given tradition has received the attention of a number of scholars, including social historians, anthropologists, and folklorists; see, for instance, Hobsbawm and Ranger (1983). According to Dean MacCannell's study of tourism (1976:14), the rhetoric of authenticity is central to the issues of tourism and display because the tourist desires experiences that are genuine.

꒜꒞

Chapter 2

Monteruju between Two Worlds

Driving north on the state road connecting Thiesi with the Carlo Felice highway, the town of Monteruju appears like a medieval crêche or a Neapolitan *presepio*.[1] Perched in a hollow halfway up an old volcanic cone, its tile-roofed houses cluster around the church steeple; its narrow, winding streets are all but invisible among the crowded buildings bordered by olive, oak, and gorse. Here and there a fold is visible, enclosed by dry stone walls and dotted with sheep. But the illusion of a former time is easily dispelled.

With a liberal administration, a population of commuters, and a growing number of retirees returning from abroad, Monteruju is very much a village of the twenty-first century. Many of its inhabitants operate computers and industrial machinery at their city jobs, then return home to milk their sheep and harvest olives. Young girls read fashion magazines and sport up-to-the-minute urban styles. Many homes are filled with televisions, refrigerators, washing machines and other modern conveniences, and parking is fast becoming a problem with the growing number of cars in the narrow streets. Still, it is not unusual to see old women swathed in black shawls on their way to or from mass, or to have one's path blocked by a shepherd on a donkey leading his flock down from the mountain, or to see a group of women washing clothing in the stream.

Life in Monteruju is marked by these contradictions—contradictions characteristic of "post-peasant" societies (Geertz, 1962:5). Clifford Geertz first coined this term to designate rural peoples in Western Europe, Japan, and Latin America whose cultures "stand in complementary relationship not to a classical great tradition . . . or a traditional hereditary elite, but to modern mass culture, a highly industrialized economy, and a thoroughly bureaucratized government" (Geertz, 1962:5), in contrast to true peasant culture, described by Redfield (1956), Wolf (1966), and others, mostly in terms of its relationship to a "great tradition" of the cultured gentry (Redfield, 1956) or economic system (Wolf, 1966).

This description applies very well today to the situation in Monteruju and, in fact, throughout much of Sardinia (Weingrod and Morin, 1973). The effects of spreading industrialization and mass culture on Italian peasant society have been described by a number of anthropologists (Pitkin, 1954; Banfield, 1958; Lopreato, 1967; Silverman, 1975).[2] Most have remarked upon the growing lack of social and organizational structures between the family and the larger society resulting from modernization. According to Geertz, no longer is there an "emphasis on strict cultural conformity as an absolute prerequisite to community acceptance; the intense degree of in-group solidarity and identification vis-á-vis *les autres*; the marked tendency towards egalitarianism, particularly on an ideological level, but to some degree on the socioeconomic, as well; the heightened consciousness of mutual dependence in terms of subsistence" (1962:14). The destruction of the traditional peasant lifestyle has brought about a corresponding change in the structure of the yearcycle and the celebration of traditional festivals themselves.

☞🍃

Background Factors

In order to better understand the changing position of festivals in the Sardinian panorama, it is necessary to briefly outline some of the background factors which have influenced Sardinian culture, and within it, the development of festivals. These include geography and climate, history, political, and linguistic issues.

Monteruju is located in northwest Sardinia, in the province of the city of Sassari, about forty kilometers from the city itself. It occupies a territory of 2,684 hectares. Located between two larger agro-towns, it is relatively isolated geographically, despite the closeness of the neighboring towns and the large city of Sassari. It is served only by a secondary road; the closest railway station is fifteen kilometers away. Daily buses connect it with Sassari and other towns in the vicinity. Its small size and isolation have kept many outsiders and tourists away, contributing to its seclusion.

Geography and Climate

The soil around Monteruju is thin and rocky, mostly a mixture of basalt and limestone; it is covered in uncultivated areas with the low-growing, scrubby vegetation typical of the Mediterranean. The climate is also characteristic of the Mediterranean, with mild, rainy winters and hot, dry summers, but subject to the unpredictability characteristic of Sardinian weather patterns (LeLannou, 1941 [1979]:48). Monteruju has two creeks that flow

The town of Monteruju

more or less year-round and serve as sources of water for washing and drinking. Summer dry spells reduce this water supply, however, and often lead to water shortages. Drought is a frequent and serious problem for both shepherds and agriculturalists.

The houses in Monteruju form a tight cluster that is completely independent from areas of agricultural activity. Individuals may own and work fields that are many kilometers from the inhabited area, necessitating a daily commute; animals are for the most part stabled in separate quarters closer to the town. This pattern, so different from the isolated farmsteads of northern Europe and America, creates a strict dichotomy between town and country, "inside" and "outside," which underlies many aspects of worldview. The habitations themselves are built of stone and mortar, with tile roofs, and are typically one or two stories high. The old part of town is built right on the slope of the old volcano and laid out in an elongated, rectangular pattern, so that the streets run uphill; the larger, more important homes are located towards the "top" of the town, near the state road. A new section of town has been developed since 1971 in the plain at the foot of the mountain. It is about one-half kilometer from the town proper and consists mostly of single-family units with yards.

The world of the villagers is bounded by geographic features to which they have given names and identities. *Su monte* is the mountain; but on the mountain there are individual stones, each with their own legends: *su carabiniere*, the policeman, a tall rock that guards the communal path up the ridge; *Tia Lukia*, Aunt Lucy, a stand of stones facing due east and said to be yellowish, like the rising sun; and *su craxtu de Funari*, the boulder of Funari, dwelling of *sa Rejusta*, a witch-like figure who emerges once a year on the night of July

31. Each bit of land in the town territory likewise has its name; a shepherd does not simply go to his lands, but *a Badde,* to The Valley, or *a Mulinu,* to The Mill, or *a sa Silva,* to The Wood. The names and stories associated with these places render the town's territory more intimately familiar to the villagers.

Monteruju is located in a larger zone called Logudoro, bordered on the north and west by the Mediterranean sea, to the east by Gallura, and to the south by Arborea (Angius, 1833:529). This area corresponds to the medieval kingdom of Torres. Villages in Logudoro tend to be small—between 500 and 5,000 inhabitants—and represent the predominant settlement pattern. Monteruju, with about 500 inhabitants, is fairly typical of many small towns in this area.

The village of Monteruju itself seems to date to the early seventeenth century, when the Spanish rebuilt it on an earlier site of a village decimated by the plague. From the scant historical record, it appears that Monteruju has had a rather stable history over the last several hundred years, with relatively little immigration from other areas of Sardinia. Most families have lived in the area for as long as anyone can remember, and the few outsiders are mostly women who have married into the village from nearby towns. In spite of this seeming cultural stability, Monteruju nevertheless has been subject to historical influences that have affected the entire island. Since "the culture of a peasant community is not autonomous; [i]t is an aspect or dimension of the civilization of which it is a part" (Redfield, 1956:68), Monteruju's history must be considered within the larger context of the history of Sardinia as a whole.

History

The history of Sardinia can best be characterized by focusing on three important concepts.[3] The first is its isolation. In spite of its position in the middle of the Mediterranean Sea, the island is isolated from the rest of the Mediterranean basin because of its distance from the mainland. Unlike Sicily, which is separated from Italy only by the narrow strait of Messina, Sardinia lies across 145 miles of ocean. This geographic isolation has contributed to certain historic phenomena, including a high degree of conservatism among island dwellers, which has led to the preservation of a number of cultural traits distinct from those of the larger Italian culture (Cirese, 1963). Although politically and economically integrated with Italy since 1860, and in spite of the homogenizing influence of the mass media, most Sardinians continue to perceive themselves as culturally distinct from mainland Italians.[4]

A second feature that deserves attention in Sardinia is the absence since medieval times of any autonomous form of government. Sardinia has always been a colony in thrall to some larger power and subject to its laws and whims. This has resulted in a marked resentment towards outsiders, whom Sardinians call "continentals," and a resistance towards influences perceived as coming from the dominant group.

A third characteristic of historical importance is the island's agrarian nature, characterized by a co-existence of agriculture and pastoralism. These two economic systems have characterized island lifestyle since Neolithic times. In spite of industrialization, Sardinia continues to be a predominantly agricultural province today; 70 percent of the population resides in centers with fewer than 20,000 inhabitants (Weingrod and Morin, 1971:302). Combined with its isolation and distrust of foreigners, this characteristic has contributed to the development of the region's distinctive culture.

Since 1948, Sardinia has been an autonomous region of Italy with its own legislature as well as representatives in the Italian parliament in Rome. The Italian government, faced with growing economic problems in the entire southern region (of which Sardinia is considered a part), has been encouraging economic development through the *Cassa per il Mezzogiorno* (Fund for the South) since 1955. Though most funding on the island has been directed towards the development of adequate irrigation and other agricultural improvements, a few attempts to institute industry have also been made. Despite government and regional efforts, Sardinia remains an economically depressed area, characterized by high unemployment and a high incidence of emigration. Politically, the region has tended to be conservative, in keeping with its strongly agricultural character. Recent years, however, have seen an upsurge in Sardinian separatist factions, which advocate regional independence from Italy. These influences, mostly concentrated in the urban centers, have brought about a renewed interest in Sardinian language, culture, and folklore; this interest is only now beginning to spread into rural areas.

Political Conflict

Monteruju is an independent *comune* (municipality) within the administrative province of Sassari and is governed by a mayor and a common council. As in many rural Italian communities, the Christian Democratic Party (D.C.) long held the majority on the council and controlled municipal affairs. But in Monteruju, for a ten-year period from 1978 to 1988, the local branch of the Italian Socialist Party (P.S.I.) gained power and held the majority on the council, initiating a series of programs and reforms based on its progressive political agenda. During this brief period, Monteruju was one of the few towns within the larger political jurisdiction of Meilogu with a socialist administration, a fact that annoyed some regional D.C. officials. While the socialist mayor and certain members of the council remained popular with voters, the P.S.I.'s majority was overturned in the elections of 1988, and the power of the D.C. was restored.

These elections were not without controversy, however. In Monteruju, political affiliation is largely a matter of family loyalty, with large or wealthy families historically holding seats on the council regardless of political ideology. In the 1988 elections, traditional family voting blocs were split in half as candidates from important families were featured on both D.C. and P.S.I. lists. The narrow victory of the D.C. nevertheless left the town reeling and riven in the wake of bitter campaigning, which had attempted to slur the personal integrity of candidates on both sides. To date, the town has not fully recovered from this rift; some previously allied families are no longer on speaking terms, and in other instances brothers have turned against sisters and fathers against their children in the continuing struggles between the D.C. and P.S.I. to administer the town's affairs. Political affiliation now colors every aspect of Monteruvians' daily lives, from one's choice of carpool members to whether or not to attend a wedding or even greet an individual one may meet on the street. This kind of conflict is not unusual in Sardinian communities (Meloni, 1984; Pinna, 1971) or even in the Mediterranean (Wylie, 1974:194–205), but it is a major determinant of individual identity and affiliation; neutrality and impartiality are not options for Monteruvians in this situation. Not surprisingly, this basic conflict is reflected in the town's two most important festivals as well.

Language

Although Italian has been the official language in Sardinia since the Piedmontese annexation, three other languages continue to be spoken on the island. These are Gallurese, a dialect of Corsican spoken in the northeastern part of the island; Catalan, spoken only in Alghero; and Sardo, spoken in the rest of the island by the vast majority of the population. Sardo[5] is considered by linguists to be distinct from Italian and other Romance languages because of a number of unique features, perhaps traceable to a pre-Roman "proto-Sardinian" (Wagner, 1951:37–38). However, like all the Romance languages, it is descended from Latin. There are three main dialect areas of Sardo: Cagliaritano, spoken in the southern half of the island; Nuorese, spoken in the central mountain area; and Logudorese, spoken in the northwestern hills. The language spoken in Monteruju belongs to this last dialect group.

The dialects share a number of common features and vocabulary but are not always mutually intelligible. For this reason, Sardinians have historically relied on the language of their conquerors to communicate with each other. Today, nearly everyone on the island understands Italian, and all but a few very old villagers speak it. Public education and the diffusion of radio and television have contributed to the spread of Italian as the official language during this century. Most official business in urban centers is conducted in Italian, and strangers will address each other in Italian until they have determined whether each other's dialects are intelligible. Sardo continues to be used heavily in rural areas. In Monteruju it is used almost exclusively, even for official business such as town council meetings and the like; and it is still the language spoken in the home and in all informal situations. But because Italian is the language of the dominant culture, a high status has come to be associated with speaking it, and a low status with speaking Sardo. Consequently, some families aspiring to middle-class status use only Italian when speaking to their children. Some individuals go as far as punishing their children if they speak Sardo. These children understand Sardo and often will even speak it with their playmates; but their parents' attitudes reinforce the general feeling that it is not a language to be valued.

In the last ten years, various movements have attempted to reinstate the status of Sardo as an independent language, to teach it in schools and adopt it as the official language in favor of Italian (Pittau, 1970). There are a number of problems with this idea, not the least of which is the determination of which dialect is to be the official one. But this plan has remained largely confined to urban, intellectual, political separatist circles and has not had much effect on rural areas, where the old values of high status/Italian and low status/Sardo persist.

🎗️☙
A Changing Economy

The economy of Monteruju has undergone radical changes in the years since the end of World War II. Before 1945, and in fact as late as the 1950s, Monteruju was mainly a farming community. The 1950 edition of the *Dizionario Enciclopedico dei Comuni d'Italia* lists its main products as "wheat, fava beans, barley, fruit and cheese" (vol. II, 589). Its economic system, which combined the cultivation of land with the use of draft animals and livestock, fits neatly into the pattern described by Eric Wolf as Eurasian grain farming and corresponds closely to his Mediterranean ecotype (Wolf, 1966, 30–32). The land was divided into two sections, one for grain cultivation, the other for livestock grazing. Durum wheat, the main crop, was planted in November so it could benefit from increased rain. Plowing was generally done with a hand-held plow drawn by oxen. If all went well, the wheat was harvested in July. Most small farmers relied on the extended family to complete the harvest; wealthy landowners could afford to hire day laborers during this period. In addition to wheat, crops such as olives, fava beans, and grapes were grown, and each household kept a few head of small livestock such as pigs or sheep and some poultry.

The most important economic change has been the decline of agriculture, accompanied by a tremendous increase in other occupations, particularly industry and service positions (see table 1). At the same time, the importance of pastoralism has greatly increased: 70 percent of households in Monteruju raise sheep. The average herd size ranges from 439 head to eight, yielding an average of 98.02 head per shepherd. The increase in shepherding is difficult to show statistically through occupation lists, however, because over 60 percent of Monteruju's shepherds actually list another occupation as their primary one. Some of these men work at other jobs during the day, often commuting to nearby towns, and tend their sheep in the early morning and late evening hours. Others are pensioners and retirees who supplement their incomes by raising sheep. The relatively small herd size reflects this occupational duality; only full-time shepherds can really manage herds of over 100

Table 1
Fathers' Occupations from Birth Records, 1866–1986*

Year	Agriculture	Shepherding	Other
1866	22	1	2
1876	22	1	4
1886	19	0	1
1896	18	2	6
1906	16	3	2
1916	10	1	2
1926	8	1	2
1936	10	0	6
1946	10	0	7
1956	10	0	2
1966	0	0	4
1976	0	0	6
1986	0	1	4
1996	0	1	3

*While this table clearly shows the decrease in agriculture as a primary economic activity and the growth of other occupations (as well as the declining birth rate), it does not show the growth of pastoralism after 1975. There are two main reasons for this: the birth rate is too low to accurately reflect occupational distribution, and many who practice shepherding list other occupations as their primary ones.
Source: Birth records, Comune di Monteruju.

head. Most shepherds in Monteruju tend their own flocks. Sons help their fathers with the work until they marry, then they usually establish a herd of their own. Only one large herd owner hires *servo-pastori* (tenant-shepherds) to tend some of his flock.[6]

The growing importance of pastoralism may be attributed to four important factors: the steady rise in milk prices, the institution of rent control on lands, the growth of the cheese industry in nearby Thiesi, and mass emigration.

Land Tenure

Prior to the 1960s, the largest tracts of land in Monteruju's territory were either privately owned or property of the township. By far the biggest part of the privately owned land was in the hands of a single titled family. Both the township and the nobles rented lands each year to the highest bidder. The nobles did not work the land themselves but instead hired day laborers and sharecroppers to work on their land. In this system, only the more prosperous shepherds—the few with substantial herds—could afford to place a high bid on the rents for pasture. The rest of the peasants, if they did not own much land themselves, hired themselves out to work for the nobles. This situation was not unique to Monteruju; it was typical of Sardinia and in fact of southern Italy as a whole. In an effort to right this situation, the Sardinian Region passed a series of laws beginning in 1966 that reduced land rents by 30 percent (Contini, 1977: I, 2591). This was followed by a similar law passed by the Italian parliament known as *DeMarzi-Cipolla* after the representatives responsible for it. The combined effect of these laws was disastrous to the landlord but very helpful to the shepherds. Suddenly it was no longer profitable for the landowning families to rent their holdings. As a result, they began to sell land in large numbers. The price of land plummeted throughout the island. Many people in Monteruju bought land at this time.

Land reform alone was not enough to change the basic economic structure of Monteruju. It coincided with two other factors that made it more profitable for these newly acquired lands to be put to use as pasture: emigration and the growing cheese industry.

Emigration and Urbanization

Emigration characterized all of southern Italy after World War II (Bianco, 1978:55). In Monteruju, there is not a single family untouched by this phenomenon. In an effort to find work in an increasingly depressed economy, many young men left the villages and migrated to the large cities in the industrial north of Italy. This large-scale internal migration, with the accompanying shift from agricultural to industrial labor, was typical of Europe during the post-war period. In Italy, those unable or unwilling to find work in the expanding Italian industries migrated to the more industrialized European nations as well as to America and Australia. This large-scale emigration left the villages depleted of able-bodied workers who in the past would have performed all the agricultural labor. Those who were left were mostly the elderly, women, and children, and those few who, for whatever reason, chose to remain in the village. Wheat, once so necessary for the maintenance of life, was no longer so now that bread and pasta were commercially available. What was needed was a cash crop that would allow the villagers to buy consumer goods with the proceeds from its sale.

Enter the nearby town of Thiesi and its complex of milk processing plants. Thiesi, like Monteruju and all the nearby communities, had once also been an agricultural center. But it is a much larger town than its neighbors—over 4,000 inhabitants—and it had always been an important market center in the area (Palmas, 1974). After the Second World War, two brothers in Thiesi founded the Casificio Pinna, a cheese manufacturing plant. Other plants followed, and Thiesi became an important financial and industrial center. The cheese plants provided an ideal outlet for sheep's milk, since they are engaged in the production and export of *pecorino*, known in the United States as Romano cheese. So it was that the new landowners in Monteruju found themselves with the perfect cash crop: one that did not require too many laborers and for which a ready market was available nearby.

Thiesi's cheese plants also employ a good many Monteruvians in labor and managerial positions, adding a further dimension to the village economy.

A number of men and women are employed in service jobs in Sassari (pop. 120,000) and commute to and from their jobs each day. Yet these people who work in factories and offices, having seemingly left behind the agricultural world of the village, remain firmly entrenched in its agrarian economic system. Many continue to raise crops and livestock on a part-time basis. In this manner, they decrease their dependence on the market economy and maintain kin ties within the village that depend on the exchange of goods and services. This type of "part-time peasant" economy is not unique to Monteruju but has been documented throughout Europe after the Second World War (Franklin, 1969; Lopreato, 1967; Hollos and Maday, 1983).

The Pastoral Year

Shepherding in Monteruju, as in other parts of the island, continues to be practiced using paleotechnic methods (Weingrod and Morin, 1971:308). Most herds are too small, and most shepherds too poor, to make the introduction of mechanized milk production worthwhile. The pastoral year begins in September, when the mature ewes and yearlings are bred. Lambs may be born at any time between December and March, with the younger ewes giving birth later. Soon after birth, those lambs not selected to continue the herd are removed from their mothers and usually slaughtered for meat. Milking for cheese production thus begins in late January or early February and continues through the summer until mating season in September. Sheep must be milked twice a day during this period. Monteruju has never had true transhumance, unlike the Barbagic area of the island. Sheep are commonly transferred from one pasture to another by their owners for various reasons, but none of the grazing lands are high enough in altitude to require a pattern of transhumance. In former times groups of shepherds would spend weeks away from the village guarding sheep in faraway pastures from thieves and raiders. The modern shepherd need not fear bandits any longer and visits his sheep twice daily by car to milk them.

Today all of the shepherds in Monteruju belong to the Cooperativa Meilogu, a cooperative buying institution that sells milk to the cheese plants in Thiesi. This cooperative was founded in 1976, as shepherding grew increasingly important in the area and local shepherds wanted to sell their milk in bulk rather than individually. Records show the growth in milk production in Monteruju in the years since the cooperative was founded (table 2).

In addition to keeping sheep, almost every family owns a few hectares used for mixed gardening, viniculture, and olive trees. The products from these lands are almost exclusively for family consumption and are seldom sold or exchanged for other goods. A few families keep other livestock as well: pigs, cows, and chickens. Horses, once indispensable for transportation, have now been replaced by automobiles. A number of people also keep donkeys, because many cultivated strips on the mountain are inaccessible by car.

Table 2
Liters of Milk Produced in Monteruju, 1976–1986

Year	Number of Liters
1976	No data available*
1977	671,680
1978	842,101
1979	620,151
1980	832,507
1981	559,180.2
1982	1,026,757
1983	1,140,376.5
1984	1,936,459
1985	1,558,858
1986	1,527,393

*The Cooperativa Meilogu was founded in 1976, and no data were available for that year.
Source: Cooperativa Meilogu.

Growing Economic Dependence

In many ways, the economic changes of the past twenty years have ended the village's isolation from the outside world. But they have also increased its dependence on the larger economic network and ended forever its days of self-sufficiency. For instance, Monteruju no longer has craftsmen and repairmen working in the village. If one needs a piece of furniture repaired or a pair of boots reheeled, one is forced to go to Thiesi or one of the other larger towns in the area. The flood of consumer goods has also sealed this bond of dependence. Plumbing, storm windows, and even radiators are now available to those building or remodeling homes, but all of the workmen and suppliers associated with these products must travel to Monteruju from larger centers. Even food acquisition is not limited to local sources: while most housewives shop daily in the tiny general store and tobacconist's shop for necessities, families also plan a weekly shopping trip to Thiesi or Sassari to buy bulk items, frozen foods, and products the small general stores cannot afford to stock. Items of clothing, household goods, and machinery must be bought outside of town, as they are simply not available in Monteruju. The advent of the automobile has facilitated this interdependence and added its own weight to the growing burden: there is no gas station in Monteruju, and the would-be traveler must first fill up in nearby Siligo or Thiesi.

Monteruju is closely linked with the outside world, not only through commercial ties but also by bureaucratic ones. After elementary school, Monteruju's children must travel to Thiesi to attend middle and high school. Students who wish to attend university must go to Sassari or Cagliari. Monteruju likewise does not have its own police force, but depends on the *carabinieri* in Siligo for protection. Similarly, all government offices outside the jurisdiction of the town council are located in Thiesi or Sassari.

This web linking the village with the other towns of Meilogu and with the city of Sassari has had a profound impact on social organization and worldview. Social interaction and marriage outside the village have been greatly facilitated and now occur more often than before. The villagers' world is no longer limited to family and neighbors—it now reaches out to include contacts in the larger world.

〜※〜

A Changing Society

We have just seen how economic changes have increased Monteruju's dependence on the world beyond its borders: nearby villages, large cities, the Italian nation, and the globe. These factors have been accompanied by transformations in Sardinian social structure and organization which also influence festival changes. They include alterations in social hierarchy, the composition of the family, and gender roles, especially as regards the role of women beyond the family.

Social Stratification and Egalitarianism

Unlike towns in other parts of southern Italy, Monteruju and other small Sardinian villages do not display great extremes of wealth and power (LeLannou, 1941 [1979]; Angioni, 1974). The historic lack in this area of large latifundia, along with the rather loose feudal organization, has contributed to the formation of a social structure different from that of the rest of southern Italy (Anfossi, 1968:227).

The social structure is characterized first of all by the absence of a local aristocracy. The descendants of feudal families, known locally as *sas damas*,[7] have long since left for the more cosmopolitan cities on the mainland. Even though they continue to own some lands, and until recently made a yearly appearance to collect rents, they do not play an important role in village life; they are perceived as outsiders. The present powerful families are descendants of landed farmers and shepherds. Wealth is measured by the possession of land, and "occupational distribution . . . [can] be charted primarily with respect to ownership of land" (Weingrod and Morin, 1971:310). At the top of the social pyramid are the *proprietari* (landowners); they are followed, in descending order, by the small landowners, tenant-farmers and shepherd share-croppers, and day laborers. However, the disparities between the large and small landowners are minimal. In the Sardinian system of land tenure, land holdings are extremely fragmented; nearly all villagers own some portion of land. "Moreover, fragmentation has become even more extreme due to the Italian system of inheritance: since according to the law all primary descendants inherit equally, the . . . lands are continually divided into smaller portions" (1971:304).

Absent, too, is a large middle class. While in the beginning of the century the middle class was composed of doctors, lawyers, merchants, teachers, and priests, this group has to a large extent deserted the village for Sassari and other island cities. Monteruju has a few merchants, a lawyer, and several teachers who might be said to constitute a kind of middle class. The lawyer and teachers really occupy a position closer to the top of the social pyramid. Unlike the large landowners, they have attained status not through land ownership but through education. Those who have acquired an education constitute what passes as the intellectual class of Monteruju, and they have held the reins of power in the community for most of this century. While in recent years a few children from modest families have managed to attend university and obtain degrees, in the past this class was a self-perpetuating group that categorically excluded nonmembers. In addition, Monteruju's class structure also includes a large number of salaried workers who continue to live in the village but whose wages come from employment elsewhere; they are mostly employed in cheese plants, construction, and service industries in Sassari. A few individuals in the village are self-employed shopkeepers.

Just as emigration to the cities has siphoned off a large part of Monteruju's middle and upper class, it has also drawn off members of the lowest socioeconomic groups: tenant farmers, shepherd sharecroppers, and day laborers. "Indeed," say Weingrod and Morin, "*braccianti* [day laborers] have to a significant degree vanished from the countryside, or are mostly represented by older men" (1971:310). Thus, one of the effects of emigration due to the industrial boom has been a leveling of the social classes within the village. But the absence of extremes of power and wealth does not in any way indicate that Monteruju's is a classless society; if anything, small differences exacerbate people's awareness of their status in the community.

Even within the existing social stratification, the actual differences in lifestyles among the classes are small. The homes of the upper-middle class do not differ drastically from those of the lower class. The traditional peasant emphasis on equality prevails; the tendency to display wealth does not exist for fear of being the object of others' hostility (Anfossi, 1968:230). This worldview has been designated by anthropologists as the concept of limited good—that is, the amount of available "good" in the community is thought to be finite, thus, one person's good exists only at somebody else's expense (Foster, 1967). A product of long-standing poverty and privation, limited good results in a cultural profile characterized by wariness and suspicion of others, a reserved and cautious approach to outsiders, and a desire to hide signs of wealth and prosperity and blend in with one's neighbors (ibid.). Where limited good is the dominant cognitive orientation, it pervades all aspects of daily life, from social status to health.

Yet the idea of limited good coexists in Monteruju with the contradictory attitude, fostered by the mass media and spread of consumer economy, of possession of certain goods as status symbols. This attitude is particularly prevalent in the younger generation. Young girls buy fashionable clothing with designer labels because of its value as a status enhancer among their peers; young men aspire to the ownership of expensive cars for the same reason. Even among the older generation, certain products are perceived as having status value.

The ultimate example of this type of behavior is found among families building or remodeling their homes. It is the current practice to furnish the house with two complete kitchens, one of which is equipped with all the most up-to-date appliances, decorator floor coverings, and so on. This kitchen is used only for entertaining and another kitchen (termed *cucina rustica* or country kitchen) for everyday cooking, eating, and socializing. The presence of a virtually unused kitchen for display purposes only points to its importance as a status symbol in the eyes of the community: it shows the family can afford modern luxuries. At the same time, the family chooses to live in the country kitchen—thus demonstrating that they do not think they deserve better than their neighbors, who perhaps cannot afford two sets of appliances. The two-kitchen household embodies perfectly the contradiction of limited good vs. status symbol in post-peasant society (cf. Dégh, 1983).

Family Ties

Most sociologists agree that the basic unit of social organization in Sardinia is the nuclear family.[8] Composed of parents and their children, it is not only a social unit but is also an economic one. In the traditional family, the father counted on his children to work and contribute to the maintenance of this unit. This is still very much the ideal in Monteruju.

Each household ideally consists of the married couple and their unmarried children. The proverb *Ogniunu a domu sua* (Everyone in his own home) expresses this ideal. Unlike peasant families in Tuscany and other parts of Europe (Falassi, 1980; Fél and Hofer, 1969), the Sardinian family does not include grandparents, children's spouses, or unmarried siblings of the husband or wife. When these situations occur, they are presented as being temporary in nature. Children continue to live at home with their parents until they marry. But because in order to marry they must have a separate dwelling from their parents and this house must be completely furnished, very late marriage age is the rule. Often a son must wait until the death of his father to inherit his share of the lands and herds before he can think of setting up an independent household. Not surprisingly, there are a large number of unmarried adults still residing at home, though they contribute financially to the maintenance of the household and in some cases support their aged parents. These bachelors and unmarried women are considered dependents until they finally marry or the parents die; in fact, they are referred to until a very late age as *piseddos* ("little ones" or "young ones").

Traditional Sardinian families are large, with as many as ten children, but family size has been decreasing steadily over the past two decades and presently averages three to six members (Anfossi, 1968:50). The smaller number of children allows for closer relationships between parents and offspring and better economic conditions for the entire family. Because of this, children in the past fifteen years have had greater educational opportunities than their predecessors did.

Under ideal conditions, the Sardinian family is thought of as an independent unit which can, and should, satisfy all its members' basic needs. However, as Angioni (1989:195ff) has argued, these ideal conditions are seldom realized. The family must maintain a network of relationships with outsiders; but ideally they should be limited to those which fulfill very specific functions. At times this ideal of rugged independence results in a kind of suspicion or distrust of nonfamilial relationships. As Pinna (1971:93) has illustrated, relationships requiring cooperation for a common good over an extended period of time are likely to be of short duration, as members quickly begin to feel resentment over real or imagined conflicts and the group splinters. Loyalty to the family is considered paramount in importance and takes precedence over any sort of friendship or parafamilial relationship. The nuclear family is the strongest unit demanding loyalty, especially before the father's death. After the death of the father, ties between siblings typically loosen somewhat and in some cases rupture altogether because of arguments over inheritance (Pinna, 1971:64–65).

In addition to the nuclear family, most people maintain ties with an extended body of relatives and parafamilial relations. Parafamilial bonds fall under the heading of *Comparatico* (fictive kinship or formalized friendship). In the case of godparenthood, a fictive kinship is contracted between two individuals, a common practice throughout the Mediterranean. Ostensibly, godparents are selected by parents to ensure a child's proper religious upbringing and to step into the parental role should the parents die or become incapacitated. A child calls his or her godparents *madrina* (godmother) and *padrino* (godfather); their relationship to the godchild is similar to that of an aunt or uncle, in that they may be called upon to provide gifts on special occasions such as christenings, first communions, graduations, and weddings. In practice, the *comparatico* formalizes bonds of friendship between the child's parents and other adults of the same gender, creating fictive kinship where no true kinship exists. Parents and godparents socialize and maintain reciprocal relationships.

In the nineteenth and early twentieth centuries, the *comparatico* often took the form of clientilism: individuals could ask wealthy or powerful landowners of the same age and gender to "co-parent" a child (Anfossi, 1968:47). By creating a fictive, but shared, relationship of responsibility, parents attempted to ensure for themselves, as well as for their children, some access to social and economic capital. A man could call upon a *compare* (literally "co-father"), or a woman upon a *comare* ("co-mother") in situations of need; the more powerful and wealthy party would then pull strings for the less powerful fictive relation. These relationships cross-cut the heavily stratified, hierarchical social structure of towns and villages, creating obligation among the wealthy and opportunities for the poor.

An interesting recent development upon which several informants commented is the present tendency for godparents to be chosen from within the family, typically from among the child's aunts and uncles. While this strengthens ties between grown siblings and cements bonds within the extended family, it does nothing to further relationships between families in the community.

Another example of comparatico is a ceremonial sanction of friendship outside the family, a practice that has been disappearing. In this form of comparatico, same-sex pairs of adolescent friends formalize their bonds of friendship in ritual, in effect declaring another form of fictive kinship. Typically, in the past, the *compares* (males) or *comares* (females) completed a ritual of knotting a handkerchief and leaping over a fire on the eve of St. John's Day (Sanna, 1970:265). One individual might have a number of friends designated as compares or comares. These relationships endure throughout an individual's life. It is unclear exactly why the comparatico has lost favor with the younger generation. Most young people have a gang of friends and several "best" friends outside the family, but they do not formalize these relationships through public ritual as their elders once did.

Relations with extended family and parafamiliars are maintained through a fairly constant exchange of gifts, visits, and favors. The principle of reciprocity dominates all social relations, but it is particularly significant within the extended family, which is considered the ideal network of social relations. Debt, as long as it is repaid and is not allowed to accumulate indefinitely, is considered beneficial to social interchange, and one enters into more debts with relatives than with people outside the extended family. It is in fact considered somewhat improper to enter into such exchanges with "strangers" (nonrelatives), as I discovered when I tried to borrow a blender from a friend. This friend was not a relative of the family with whom I was staying, and my "family" therefore prevented me from borrowing the appliance from her. Instead, I was directed to a cousin who also had the requisite appliance. The important point about this interchange is that while this young woman was perfectly willing to lend me her blender, my "family" was not willing to allow me to enter into a relationship of reciprocity with a nonrelative.

Gender Roles

Gender roles within the traditional Sardinian family are quite clearly defined. The women's sphere is the home and everything having to do with the running of the household, including the processing of agricultural and pastoral products; the men's sphere is work outside the home, including agricultural labor and the tending of the flocks. Before the diffusion of the automobile, men were often absent from the village for weeks at a time, tending their flocks on the mountain or working fields that were located far away from the inhabited areas. This left women in the village with considerable autonomy, especially in the realm of social relations. While men's labor tends to isolate them from one another, women's work brings together relatives, neighbors, and friends, forming the nucleus of reciprocity networks which are important to village life. Women thus tend to be seen as responsible for the maintenance of social relations within the village.

Until very recently, segregation of the sexes was the rule in nearly all work and social activities from childhood to adulthood. Even when men and women are working together on one activity, such as the olive harvest, each will have a distinct task and role: men climb the trees to shake down the olives, while women kneel on the ground to gather them (cf. Brandes, 1980).

Most women see marriage and motherhood as their primary goals. Because a couple must have their own house before getting married, late marriage is the rule; few men marry before the age of forty, few women before age thirty. The traditional marriage was an economic arrangement characterized by an absence of the concept of romantic love and its attendant problems (Anfossi, 1968:48). The ideal marriage was endogamous and between strict status equals, though it was tolerable if the man had higher status than the woman. The present-day ideal is quite different. In fact, the introduction of the concept of romantic love may be one factor contributing to the decreasing marriage rate among young Monteruvians. While in earlier times a woman may have been happy to marry a man who was a good provider, a "serious person," contemporary young women want someone quite different: "I want above all a person I can talk to," one woman told me. But the worlds of men and women are still so separate that it was unclear to me at the time exactly what she and her hypothetical future husband would talk about.

This dilemma is heightened by the educational discrepancy between young men and women. While most young men drop out of school after finishing the mandatory nine years of free education, many young girls continue on to obtain their diplomas in various areas such as nursing, accounting, and teaching. Few of these young women find a life of hard labor (processing cheese and other pastoral products) very appealing. They desire middle-class, white-collar husbands whose lifestyle more closely matches their own ideals than that of the shepherds and construction workers their schoolmates have become.

The young men who do choose to continue their education usually leave the community for the greener economic pastures of the mainland. Fewer young women leave home permanently, perhaps because most young women continue to see themselves in terms of their relationships to others in their families, despite the occasional conflicts in values and worldview. Also, unmarried women continue the traditional pattern of remaining at home to care for their aged parents (Da Re, 1989). The present situation is therefore one of great educational and cultural disparity between men and women aged 20 to 40. This has resulted in a low marriage rate in this age group and has tended to undercut traditional endogamous marriage patterns.

While at one time endogamous marriages were the rule, they are now decreasing in favor of exogamous marriages, facilitated by the growing contact with outside communities (see table 3). In most cases, women are the ones who leave their communities to settle in the villages of their new hus-

Table 3
Marriage Patterns in Monteruju, 1866–1986

Year	Marriages within Monteruju	Marriages Outside Monteruju
1866	4	2
1876	2	3
1886	4	1
1896	3	0
1906	3	2
1916	0	0
1926	3	1
1936	5	3
1946	3	2
1956	2	2
1966	1	1
1976	2	1
1986	0	0
Increase in Marriages Outside the Community, 1980–1986		
1980	2	5
1981	1	2
1982	0	6
1983	0	4
1984	1	1
1985	1	2
1986	0	0

Source: Marriage records, Comune di Monteruju.

bands. Although these marriages strengthen the ties between towns, they weaken family and social ties within the community itself. In many cases, women marrying into the village from outside communities remain virtual outsiders in Monteruju, even after many years of residence.

Within the nuclear family, the father is usually presented as the highest authority. Yet the mother's role is not necessarily devoid of power. Her influence over her husband is usually such that she has considerable say in most matters, especially those pertaining to the household and the rearing of children. In some families, her role can be very powerful; Marta Pinna explained, "My father brought home the wages, but it was my mother who administered them." Sometimes the mother is also the only one who has a mitigating effect on the father's authority and is thus called in to mediate conflicts between father and children: as Elena Tanca told me, "Mother was the only one who could ever talk any sense into my father." Elena's father was particularly authoritarian; after her mother's death, the children were left at the mercy of his whims, making her loss even more poignant.

Even in less extreme cases, the mother is always the emotional center of the family, and children usually feel closer to their mother than to their father.

Rita Solinas, whose father had recently died, said: "Dad's death was terrible, but it wasn't as if we'd lost our mother. Mama is sweetness, love, everything." This recalls Angioni's observation that "[t]he household is the height of humanity. And the woman within the household is almost everything, as if the house were an extension of her body as mother and wife, daughter or sister who is 'in charge' of the house" (Angioni, 1989:206). Because the woman's position within the household is so central to the family, a high value is placed on the woman's physical proximity to the home. The ideal is for women not to have to perform agricultural labor in the fields, and women almost never tend sheep. While many women work for wages before marriage, most cut back their hours or leave salaried positions altogether once they marry and have children.

The home is thus a reflection of the woman and her abilities as a homemaker. Ideally, it is kept spotlessly clean and orderly. Even young women who work outside the home are heavily criticized for not conforming to the society's ideal of the woman as homemaker. One 27-year-old woman told me the reason she decided to attend the university was primarily "so I wouldn't have to stay home and clean."

Changing Women's Roles

In spite of the still-high level of segregation of the sexes and the prevailing traditional model of women's roles, the position of women in society has nevertheless changed a great deal in the past thirty years.[9] Women today have greater educational opportunities than their mothers, due to the availability of public education, shrinking family size, and improved economic conditions. Much more personal freedom is available to women as well. Many women now in their fifties and sixties spoke of oppressive family control over their lives in their youth. "When I was a girl, it wasn't like it is now," said one 54-year-old woman. "We had to remain in the house; the most we could do was huddle on the doorstep. If my father caught us going out further, he would beat us." Today, teenage girls commonly come and go as they please during the day and often at night, too, when they visit nearby towns with friends to attend movies, discos, or festivals.

The differences between the pre-war and post-war generations of women are striking, even among siblings raised in the same family. Whereas most women born before 1945 do not work outside the home, did not receive education beyond the elementary level, and retain traditional modes of dress and hairstyle, women born after this date are less conservative in their habits. They are typically more educated, having received at least a junior high diploma, and wear their hair cut short rather than braided and pinned up at the nape of the neck like their mothers. Their clothing style is apt to reflect current fashions (in 1989 these included miniskirts, sweatshirts with logos in English, and Timberland shoes), and they typically do not adhere to the custom of wearing black as a sign of mourning at the death of a close relative.

This generation of women is also more likely to work (or have worked at one time) outside the home, often in typically feminine jobs (e.g., domestic, nurse, schoolteacher). Compared to their older sisters, they show a marked degree of autonomy from their families. These differences naturally lead to conflicts between generations, particularly between parents, who remember other standards of behavior for women, and daughters, who wish to conform to a new cultural pattern diffused through the mass media. While few parents begrudge their daughters an education or a job (particularly when this contributes to the family's income), conflicts typically center around the young woman's free time. Many parents feel this should be spent at home, while most girls prefer to spend at least some of their spare time away from home with their friends or at nearby discos and bars. Since in former times this behavior on the part of a woman was tantamount to promiscuity, the family squabbles on this issue are endless.

There is some evidence that these changes are resulting in decreasing sex segregation. In the generation presently in its teens, for instance, there is much greater contact between males and females than was once customary. Teenage boys and girls hang out together after school, in front of the bar or in the public reading room. Moreover, many cultural expectations once reserved for young boys now apply equally to girls, particularly those having to do with education and work outside the home. And, significantly for this study, the once single-sex festival committees have been altered to include both men and women since 1979. The following chapters discuss this development in detail.

There is little doubt that women's increased social status is due in great part to their growing economic power. A significant number of women below the age of forty are employed outside the home. In Monteruju in 1985, three local business establishments were owned and operated by women. Many women have nursing degrees and are employed in hospitals in Sassari, while some are schoolteachers. A number work in offices as clerical workers, and many have part-time jobs as domestic helpers. Today there are several university-educated women in Monteruju, and a number of others are attending university in pursuit of degrees. Women's influence extends to the political sphere, as well: Monteruju's town council has seven women councilors, about evenly split between the D.C. and the P.S.I., and the area's first woman mayor.

While no one would argue that women in Monteruju have achieved status equal to that of men, and while the majority of women, including those working outside the home, continue to hold traditional ideals of womanhood connected to marriage and motherhood, the growing influence of women in many spheres of life has had an important effect on gender relations in the village, heightening the conflict between women and men. This conflict is reflected in the structure and organization of the festivals examined in the following chapters.

🎀

Society and Conflict in Monteruju

Monteruvian society does not exist as a monolithic whole; rather, as we have seen, it is composed of individuals, families, and family groups whose interests often conflict. The most apparent conflict at this moment is political; but one can also detect evidence of class, gender, and generational conflict. These conflicts find expression in the organization and performance of festivals.

Increasing Isolation of the Nuclear Family

The Sardinian family has long been able to maintain its ideals of independence because of social networks, kept up largely by women, which created a web within which the family could operate. However, recent years have seen an increasing isolation of the family, due in part to the continued pursuit of the independent ideal and in part to social and economic conditions that have made that ideal easier to attain, on one level. Yet these transformations have also led to the breakdown of groups and occasions which functioned as vehicles for intrafamilial socialization. I have already noted the tendency to appoint godparents from within the ranks of close kin as a practice that has removed one type of intrafamilial tie from the society, as well as the increasing incidence of exogamous marriage. But there are other forces working to increasingly isolate the Monteruvian family from the network that once supported it, and to link it up, ultimately, with the broader world outside the village. Neighborhood groups, informal friendships, religious organizations, and work groups once forced contact between families and individuals, even those who were in conflict. The breakdown of some of these groups has meant that conflicts split the community more readily and are more difficult to heal.

The Neighborhood Group

In the days before the advent of modernization in the 1960s, the neighborhood group—an informal association among families living in contiguous habitations—was an important vehicle for socializing outside the kin group. Usually formed in childhood from groups of children living near one another who habitually played together in the street, the feelings of solidarity engendered by these groups tend to persist into adulthood. Boys who once played together become young men who hang out at the bar together and older men who drink together. Among women, if a relative were not available to help with some task, the next best individual to ask has always been a neighbor. In the days when women baked once a week in wood ovens, neighborhood groups often formed around this activity: everyone knew who was baking when, and neighbors would come over asking to put a dish of vegetables or a rabbit in the oven with the bread. Firing one's own oven for such small tasks was considered wasteful. The woman "lending" the oven was usually "repaid" by being offered a bit of the cooked food.[10]

Ironically, modernization has increased the self-sufficiency of each household and has led to less interdependence between neighbors. Each housewife now has her own gas oven, which she uses daily in cooking, as well as other appliances that make borrowing from neighbors obsolete. *"Ogni-uno a casa sua; ogniuno per conto suo"* (Each one in his own home; each one on his own) is how one older woman informant expressed this new lifestyle. The ideal isolation of each individual household is perfectly reflected in the layout of the new section of town, where houses do not share contiguous walls as they do in the old village but instead stand isolated from one another, sur-rounded by a yard or fenced garden.

Work Groups

Work groups, like neighborhood groups, were based on mutual depen-dence. Certain seasonal activities such as corn shucking, sheep shearing, olive harvesting, and making *cicciones* (a traditional form of pasta) required more hands than a single family could supply. On these occasions, it was the custom for several families to get together and help each other reciprocally. These get-togethers were the prime occasions for the exchange of *contasscias*, a catchall term used to refer to narrative genres.[11] Although some forms of cooperative labor persist, the agricultural economy that provided the base products around which these activities revolved no longer exists, and work parties are less common now than they used to be.

Religious Organizations

Like many other Italian communities, at one time Monteruju had a num-ber of religious organizations in the form of religious fraternities and sorori-ties. The main role of these societies was the direction and organization of religious manifestations surrounding the week before Easter (Satta, 1982:137). The fraternity (*cuffrates*) undertook the tasks requiring physical strength, while the sorority (*cusorres*) was in charge of the ceremonies surrounding the dress-ing of the statues of the Virgin and Christ, which were carried in procession. Participation in these para-religious organizations conferred social status to the individual; cuffrates and cusorres marched in all the religious processions of the year-cycle. In large towns, this social power could sometimes extend to the political sphere, but in Monteruju the confraternities remained under the guidance and control of the local priest.

Religious confraternities were abolished in 1962 by papal decree, and as the waves of change and protest of the 1960s began to reach even Monteruju, membership in the Catholic youth organizations gradually fizzled out. For a time, they were replaced by discussion groups of a political nature (involving both men and women), but eventually these, too, faded, leaving no formal youth organizations in their place.

Friendship

Informal friendships, of course, exist between individuals; these are par-ticularly important during adolescence. Teenage girls and boys each have a group of same-sex friends with whom they spend leisure hours, usually outside the bar or in the public reading room. While males may continue such friendships into adulthood and past marriage, most women grow increasingly distant from their girlfriends after marriage. Their role as mothers and housewives permits social exchange with female relatives, but not with those outside the family. Friendships unite groups of adult males within the community but are not always carried over to include the entire family. Male friendships are commonly solidified through activities, such as shared drinking, which are out of the sphere of women and children. Thus, while friendships may unite select groups within the community (e.g., adolescents, adult males), they do little on the whole to bind the village together on a more global level.

It should be clear from the preceding discussion that recent changes have actually lessened the occasions for interfamily contact and socialization in Monteruju. As economic well-being becomes more accessible, the need for borrowing from relatives and neighbors decreases; or, more significantly, the willingness to borrow and thus admit need and enter into a state of indebtedness with the lender has decreased. The ideal model of the independent nuclear family has isolated the family unit to a great degree from participation in the village's social network. Gone, too, are communal work parties, which used to be festas in and of themselves, and parareligious organizations that provided additional occasions for socializing. The festival organizing committees are one of the few remaining community groups in which Monteruvians participate, outside family life and informal friendships, which provide opportunities for interchange on an organized level.

Amidst such sweeping, fundamental changes in lifestyle, values, and worldview, the traditional ritual year-cycle, so closely tied to the agro-pastoral year-cycle, could not continue to exist unchanged.

꿍ᵕ

A Changing Identity

Due to growing economic dependence on outside communities and decreasing community solidarity, Monteruju's sense of identity is undergoing a period of crisis. Monteruju's small size and isolation have given it a feeling, seldom articulated but often sensed, of being less sophisticated than its neighbors. Monteruvians are extremely self-conscious about this, and for many years the town did its best to modernize, to "keep up with the Joneses," as it were, in neighboring towns. Many Monteruvians commented on how quickly certain traditional customs, including calendar customs, were discarded in comparison to other towns. While at one time this was a mark of pride, now that they are gone there is a widespread nostalgia for them as cultural symbols. With its identity threatened both within and without, the desire to return to symbols of another time is inevitable.

In folklore and blason populaire, Monteruju has long suffered from an undeserved reputation for being more "backwards" and rustic than other towns in the area. Francesco Enna (1984) collected from a tale teller in nearby Siligo the well-known European numbskull tale of the fools who mistake a field of flax for the sea (AT 1290) and the fool who forgets to count himself (AT 1287). In these variants, the fools are said to be from Monteruju (Enna, 1984:21). Not enough evidence is available to determine whether the designation of Monteruvians as fools was a choice of the individual tale teller or a part of the local tradition. While not renowned as a community of fools as is, for example, Sorso, it is nevertheless significant that the tale teller or local tradition characterized Monteruvians as foolish and gullible.

The slurs associated with Monteruju likewise emphasize its backwards quality in comparison to its neighbors. Thiesi, the nearest large town, has always been known for its economic power and the business sense of its inhabitants. According to an unverifiable local legend that clearly reflects the traditional European ethnic slur, it was founded by a colony of Jews (Palmas, 1971:4–8). The inhabitants of Siligo, the nearest town to Monteruju, are often characterized by the saying *Silighesos, bragosos*, which can be roughly translated as "Silighesi, braggarts." According to one informant they are consumed by the desire to excel and distinguish themselves in some way. Another characterized them as proud. The prominent Silighesi Gavino Ledda (author of *Padre, Padrone*) and singer Maria Carta are often cited as living proof of the stereotype. The inhabitants of Banari are characterized by their visceral enthusiasm; it is said that they never do anything halfway; that they are hot-tempered, passionate, and prone to fighting.

About Monteruju, however, the popular stereotype says only *pes mannos*, "big feet." None of my informants could give a satisfactory explanation for this characteristic. One woman said she had heard it used by a shoe salesman in the market, who remarked to a mother buying her son some shoes that the boy was typical of Monteruvians because he had big feet. The slur is meant, then, in quite a literal way. Large feet suggest a roughness and lack of refinement characteristic of peasants who spend most of the year barefooted, as in fact many Monteruvians did before the Second World War. The slur is intended to underscore the backwards, rural, and impoverished image of the town that seems to be current in the area.

Monteruvians are understandably sensitive about the image of their town and, in part to belie it, have always hosted lavish festivals to display their resources to their neighbors. But, as we will see in the following chapter, the consumerization of the festival has made the lavishness of former years inaccessible to small communities with a weak economic base, striking yet another blow at Monteruju's identity and self-image.

Notes

[1] The *presepio* or *presepe* is a representation of the nativity of Jesus, usually associated with the Christmas celebration. The first presepio is attributed to St. Francis of Assisi in 1223. By 1400,

the habit of constructing presepi in churches had diffused throughout Italy but was especially popular in the south. Elaborate Renaissance and Baroque presepi reproduce in miniature entire Italian villages from the period in accurate detail, of which the actual scene of the holy family at the manger is only a small part. Studies of this tradition include Hager (1902), Musumarra (1957), and Stefanucci (1944).

2 Banfield (1958) was one of the earliest to describe what he interpreted as the isolation of the family in a Calabrian village; he called this "amoral familism." Unfortunately, his work is flawed by a lack of historical depth, scant knowledge of the language, and, worst of all, a moralistic stance, wherein Calabrian society is unfavorably compared to that of a typical New England town in the 1950s. The application of Banfield's findings to Sardinia has been criticized by Pinna (1971) and Meloni (1984).

3 To date, no comprehensive history of Sardinia is available in English. For the most comprehensive history of the island, see Carta Raspi (1971). For Sardinian prehistory, see Lilliu (1963); for the Roman period, see Meloni (1975). Bellieni (1973) gives a history of medieval Sardinia in three volumes; see also Boscolo (1978), Paulis (1983), and Artizzu (1985).

4 In this, Sardinia is analogous to other regions within European nations that perceive themselves as culturally distinct from the national culture. For a discussion of the same process in Brittany, for example, see McDonald (1989).

5 A comprehensive grammar of Sardinian, with attention to all the basic dialect groups, has yet to be developed. The seminal work on the origins, development, and characteristics of the Sardinian language remains Wagner (1951). Wagner (1960) is the most comprehensive and thorough dictionary of the language.

6 For a comprehensive description of the practice of pastoralism in Sardinia, see Angioni (1989).

7 Sas damas means, literally, "the ladies," but in Monteruju this term was used to refer to members of noble families regardless of their gender.

8 A number of sociologists have examined the impact of recent economic changes on the social organization of Sardinian towns. Some of the best-known works include Anfossi (1968), Pinna (1971), and Meloni (1984). Of these, Pinna discusses, albeit briefly, the important role of festivals in the social life of the town. According to him, these festivals and seasonal rituals "seem to uncover and expose for all to see the entire affective chain linking together the whole community. . . . Through the ritualization of social relations, the traditional community is able to control its internal tensions and thus maintain its cohesion" (Pinna, 1971:15).

9 Traditional women's roles in Sardinian society have been studied by Atzeni (1988), Da Re (1990), and Murru Corriga (1989). These works examine traditional divisions of labor, marriage patterns, and family roles in pre-industrial Sardinia. A collection of essays by various authors (Cecaro et. al., 1989) examines more closely the effects of social transformation on women in the northern part of the island, including areas around Monteruju. For an excellent recent overview of changing women's roles over three generations, see Assmuth (1998).

10 A number of amusing anecdotes center around this now-defunct custom, most revolving around some nonedible animal being baked in a woman's oven without her knowledge. When she finally tasted a morsel of the dish and pronounced it good, the perpetrators began to laugh and imitate the behavior of the animal to give away the joke. Usually it is a cat that has been baked in the guise of a rabbit.

11 Contasscias is a catchall term Monteruvians use to refer to many narrative genres. It seems to include all types of folktales and perhaps also legends, although not enough evidence is available at this time to precisely delineate this native terminology. For a collection of Sardinian contasscias with a side-by-side Italian translation, see Enna (1984).

Chapter 3

Festivals in Sardinia
History and Organization

In Sardinia, events such as the celebration of the Assumption or Santa Maria di Runaghes are called *festas*. Festas are, first and foremost, celebrations. In Sardinia as in all of Italy, festas usually celebrate and honor a saint or an important event in the Roman Catholic liturgical year. Festas thus have religious as well as secular components.

What we call festivals and Monteruvians call festas have been studied under a variety of names: calendar customs and year-cycle rites are two terms favored by early scholars who noticed a number of features common to these phenomena and tried to account for them. Nineteenth-century scholars such as Wilhelm Mannhardt (1875) first noticed that the celebrations of European peasants coincided with important times in the agricultural cycle, such as sowing and harvesting. This observation led to the widespread belief that festivals were in fact the detritus of ancient pagan fertility rites, a theory embraced by certain scholars of Sardinian festival (Petazzoni, 1912; Lanternari, 1984) and now popularized again by the tourist market in an attempt to lure people into vicariously experiencing the ancient past.[1] While scholars have become skeptical of these historic generalizations, festivals and celebrations are undoubtedly tied to the economy of the areas in which they are observed. Usually, festivals take place either at times of agricultural or economic plenty or during periods of relative inactivity in the agricultural year cycle.[2]

Festivals also have a strong ritual component. It was Arnold van Gennep who first identified festivals as rites of passage (van Gennep, 1909). According to his theories, ceremonies and celebrations which take place annually, seasonally, monthly, or even daily help societies negotiate the sometimes difficult transitions from season to season, from one period of the year to another. These ceremonies, or year-cycle rites as he called them, take place at

39

critical junctures during the agricultural year, when anxiety about the outcome of agricultural labor runs high. Participating in the celebrations soothes group anxiety, according to van Gennep, and often serves a propitiatory function: the group makes offerings to some higher power in hopes of achieving a desired outcome in return. Each community's year cycle contains a number of year-cycle rites.

Most folklorists agree that European year-cycle rites and celebrations have historical roots in the practices of ancient peoples who settled throughout Europe in prehistoric times. Through time and contact with new cultures and civilizations, these practices changed; individuals and groups retained elements they liked and found meaningful and jettisoned others which were no longer significant. Older elements were often reinterpreted in light of new ideologies, giving them layer upon layer of meaning. Most European year-cycle rites now contain a mixture of elements built upon a pre-Christian substratum that has been christianized and influenced by many subsequent historical and social movements.

Festivals in Sardinia are typical of this pattern. Their oldest roots are in the customs of the earliest colonizers of the island, a Neolithic Mediterranean people who dug shaft tombs into steep basalt and limestone cliffs and erected large dolmens on holy sites. They were followed by settlers who erected huge dry stone fortifications known as *nuraghi* and built holy wells out of ashlar masonry on the sites of springs. While archeologists disagree about whether nuraghi were connected with cult practices, it is not uncommon to find archeological continuity in many of these sites: shaft tombs, the remains of a nuraghe or holy well, and a Christian chapel on the same location (Lanternari, 1984). Since chapels are the common location for festivals, it is tempting to believe that a direct link exists between the practices of the earliest Sardinians and the festivals they celebrate today.

But Sardinia has had numerous intervening cultural influences. During a lengthy period of Roman domination the Roman state religion was adopted throughout the island; gods and goddesses from the Roman pantheon were worshipped. It was in the late Roman period that Christianity was introduced to the island, which the Romans used as a dumping ground for Christian exiles. During the early medieval period, the Byzantines introduced numerous Greek elements into the language, culture and religion of Sardinia. Some scholars see the celebration of the Assumption and the widespread horse races associated with many Sardinian festivals as Byzantine legacies (Paulis, 1983). Later occupations by the Italian maritime republics and the Spaniards introduced additional practices into the popular religion of the islanders. Each successive colonizer left a distinctive cultural stamp upon the practices and customs of the island. The resulting year cycle is characteristic and unique to itself, differing markedly from the classic Italian pattern.[3]

🐦🐦

The Traditional Year Cycle

The traditional Sardinian year cycle has been described in detail by a number of scholars (Costa, 1911:60–95; Bottiglioni, 1925:24–90; Delitala, 1963:294–300; Satta, 1982). The pastoral and ritual year traditionally began on September 1 in Sardinia. The Sardinian name for this month, *Kapidanni*, is derived from the Latin *caput anni*, "the head of the year" (Costa, 1911:62). Rent contracts for land and pasture were settled at this time and ran from September 1 to August 31 of the following year. The first festival of the year in Monteruju was thus Santa Maria di Runaghes, observed on September 8, the day of the Nativity of the Blessed Virgin. This festival ushered in the fall/pre-winter cycle, which included the observances of Michaelmas (September 29), All Saints and All Souls (November 1 and 2), and in Monteruju culminated in a large festival in honor of Monteruju's co-patron, St. Martin, on November 11. St. Martin was celebrated in much the same way as the Feast of the Assumption, Monteruju's second patronal festival, on August 15. The two dates in fact perfectly frame the agricultural year: St. Martin roughly corresponded to the period of the sowing of wheat, while the Assumption took place immediately following the harvest and threshing of the grain.

The early winter cycle included the festivities surrounding Christmas, St. Sylvester (December 31), and the Epiphany (January 6). Christmas celebrations in Monteruju and throughout Sardinia centered around the family; this was a time to weld and strengthen family bonds (Satta, 1982b:19). Midnight mass on December 24 and Christmas dinner were the two main points of the celebration (Costa, 1911:67). Celebrations were characterized by an abundance of food, especially roasted meats (which at one time were seldom eaten during the rest of the year), and elaborated versions of everyday foods such as pasta, breads, and soups (Satta, 1982:24–26). Families attended midnight mass together. Customs surrounding St. Sylvester and New Year's Day on January 1 are of recent introduction, as the new year was once celebrated in September (Costa, 1911:67). The night of December 31, known as *sa notte de bennaldzu* (the January night), was a time for prognostications to determine the nature of the harvest during the coming year and a woman's marriage prospects (Sanna, 1969:171). Shepherds invited their families to a feast in the folds consisting of roasted lamb, piglet, and lamb innards, accompanied by *sa kottsula in tonte*, bread with the drippings from the roasted meat. The night of January 6, the Epiphany, was an occasion for ritual door-to-door begging in Sardinia; adult males and young people of both sexes participated in the *quête*, asking for food and drink. The proceeds from the begging were divided among the *quêting* group and taken home to share with family members (Sanna, 1969:198–236).

The late winter cycle began with the celebration of St. Giuliano on January 9. This holiday was later removed from Monteruju's sacred calendar, and no data were available on its celebration. St. Sebastian, once observed on Jan-

uary 20, was moved early in this century to the middle of May by a committee of shepherds who served as organizers. This was a *festa de komitatu*
(committee festival), observed by those who had made a vow to the saint but
not by the community as a whole. The late winter cycle culminated with the
observance of Carnival on the Tuesday preceding the beginning of Lent.

As in all of Europe, Carnival was characterized by a reversal of ordinary
norms of behavior and a leveling of class distinctions. Both male and female
informants recalled cross-sex dressing and participating in elaborate pranks.
The carnival figure in Monteruju and the surrounding area is known as *Jolzi*
(George); Costa connects him with the Byzantine cult of St. George, as well
as with *verde Giorgio* ("green George," cf. English Jack in the Green), a figure
dressed in green leaves and connected, perhaps, to a vegetation deity (Costa,
1911:72–73). A dummy-figure Jolzi was paraded through the town by young
men, then finally burned or stabbed to death. The figure often concealed a
bag of wine, which would burst upon its demise, showering spectators with
"blood"/wine.

The spring of the year was marked by the observance of Easter and
included the period between Palm Sunday and Easter Monday. Religious fraternities were involved in all aspects of the Easter rite, which included the ritual meeting of the statues of the dead Christ and the Madonna in a
procession around the village (Satta, 1982:127–143). Easter was an important
occasion for social interchange, both within the context of the religious confraternities and the family; a large number of sweets were prepared for
exchange with friends, family, and neighbors on this occasion. The festivities
of Easter ended the abstinence of Lent and marked the renewal of life in the
natural world as well as the liturgical one.

Most of Sardinia lacks a ritual tradition surrounding May 1 (Satta,
1982b:127). The end of the spring season and the beginning of the summer
were marked by the observance of the feasts of St. Anthony of Padua on June
13 and St. John the Baptist on June 24. St. Anthony was thought of locally as
the patron saint of young people, and his festa was organized by a committee
of unmarried young men. The Eve of St. John the Baptist, just following the
summer solstice, marked the peak of the growing season. This important day,
observed throughout Italy and Europe, was thought to be particularly appropriate for gathering medicinal herbs. Water on this day was thought to
acquire magical properties and to become "holy" (Costa, 1911:86; Sanna,
1969:283), capable of healing disease. In Monteruju, the magic in the water
was known as *su balsamu* and was characterized as an oily or slippery sub-
stance. Persons of all ages ritually bathed in the creeks on the eve of June 24,
as su balsamu was thought to have healing properties. On St. John's Eve,
bonfires were lit on street corners and in the countryside, and those who
wished could become compares or comares (fictive kin) by reciting a formula
while tying knots in a handkerchief, then leaping over the flames (Sanna,
1969:265). Similar bonfires were lit for Sts. Peter and Paul on the night of
June 28.

The harvest and the end of the growing season were celebrated through-out the island with the Feast of the Assumption, while the observance of the Nativity of the Virgin on September 8 inaugurated the new agro-pastoral year.

꽃ﾉ꿩

The Year Cycle Today

The economic and social changes of the past thirty years have been paral-leled by significant changes in the observance of traditional year-cycle cus-toms. Since most year-cycle rites were at one time linked with the agricultural year, and agriculture has declined dramatically in Sardinia, it is not surpris-ing that many year-cycle rites have declined or disappeared altogether. The old year cycle in Monteruju paralleled the agro-pastoral year, framed by the two festivals which are the focus of this study. But there have been a number of changes in the observance of year-cycle customs in the last thirty years, and many of them have declined or disappeared entirely. The touristicization of the Assumption and the revival of Santa Maria di Runaghes must be understood within the context of these changes.

Like the festa of Santa Maria di Runaghes, which ceased to be celebrated for a short time, a number of saints' days have simply ceased to be observed in Monteruju. St. Michael and St. Giuliano have not been observed since the 1920s, and the celebration of St. Anthony was discontinued after the Second World War, when because of the mass emigration too few boys were left behind to carry on the tradition. The observance of Sts. Peter and Paul on June 29, which involved the custom of lighting bonfires, has also ceased in Monteruju. Gone, too, are a number of customs associated with important days in the year cycle. The ritual begging associated with the Epiphany ceased to be practiced around 1970;[4] the Epiphany has now become another occasion for children to receive gifts from the witch *la Befana*, as it is in Italy. The ritual bathing associated with St. John the Baptist is no longer practiced, and only one small ritual fire was lit by a group of mischievous boys in 1986 and was quickly extinguished. The ceremonies of the religious fraternities surrounding Easter week were prohibited by the Church in 1962 and have not been practiced in Monteruju since.[5] Only a few children observe Carnival by dressing in costumes and making a Jolzi out of old clothes to drag through the streets; most teenagers and young adults prefer to travel to another com-munity to observe the festivities.

A number of other customary observances have been modified through contact with the mass media and their portrayal of the ideals of the dominant culture. St. Sylvester, December 31, is now characterized by celebrations modeled on fashionable middle-class festivities portrayed on television, with champagne, toasts, dancing, and feasting in restaurants. The Italian custom of inaugurating the new year by shooting firearms or throwing old crockery out the window has replaced the weather and love prognostications of the past.

An interesting phenomenon in the evolution of the year cycle is the increasing touristicization of traditional year-cycle observances. With the spread of the automobile and the resulting facilitated transportation, traditional year-cycle customs have become occasions for tourism and display. The result is that few small towns have preserved the multitude of rich year-cycle observances which once characterized peasant life. What is happening instead is a kind of specialization by town in one particular custom or saint's day celebration, which is turned into a display event for the attraction of tourists from other towns. Increasingly, year-cycle customs such as St. John the Baptist (June 24), Carnival, and St. Anthony (January 17), which as recently as 1969 were still actively observed in Monteruju and neighboring communities (Sanna, 1969), are now observed mostly by traveling to other towns where they have become huge tourist display events. St. John the Baptist is observed by driving to Mores to watch the ritual bathing, bonfire, and fireworks display; Carnival is celebrated by watching the parades in Tempio, the *Sartiglia* (traditional display of horsemanship) in Oristano, or the traditional festivities in Bosa (Satta, 1982b:114–119; Counihan, 1985). The same mechanism is at work in Monteruju in the growing folklorization and touristicization of the Feast of the Assumption.

It is significant to note that in traveling to other communities to watch year-cycle rites, one goes as a spectator to be entertained, not as a participant. Those who travel to Mores for St. John, for instance, do not themselves engage in ritual bathing but merely watch those who do; those attending Carnival celebrations in other towns do not wear costumes or participate in the parade but stand at the sidelines watching the local participants. The lack of active participation and the clear role of the tourists as spectators mark the transformation of the year-cycle custom into a consumer product; the custom is reduced to a show or spectacle, losing some of its former affective charge (Mesnil, 1987:192). The yearly television broadcasts of such year-cycle customs as Oristano's Sartiglia and the *ardia* (horse race) in Sedilo in honor of the patron saint Constantine (July 7) contribute to the transformation of these events into consumer products.[6] It has become possible now to "observe" year-cycle rites from the comfort of one's living room without even leaving Monteruju. "Why do you go all the way to Bonorva for Carnival, when you could stay here at home and watch the Sartiglia on television?" one mother asked her daughters in an attempt to persuade them not to go out.

The transformation of the year-cycle rite into tourist display event, coupled with the readiness of many young people to seek entertainment outside the community on traditionally significant days, has contributed to the shrinking opportunities for interaction on a community level in Monteruju. In fact, even when such opportunities exist, there is an unwillingness to interact on a local level. The following incident, which occurred at Carnival in 1986, clearly illustrates this circumstance.

On this year, Carnival took place on February 11 and was marked in many parts of the island by record snowfall. The roads connecting Monteruju with the outside world were blocked by snow and ice and were rendered impassable. Many who were planning to attend celebrations in Tempio, Bosa, Oristano, or even in the nearby towns of Thiesi and Bonorva unexpectedly found themselves stuck in Monteruju. In order to make the best of the situation and allay disappointment, the owner of the bar and a number of other young men decided to organize an impromptu party for everyone in the old school building. They approached Bruna, a 26-year-old unmarried woman and the local librarian, and some of her friends, and asked them to make *frittelle* (traditional carnival sweets of fried dough) for the party. But the young women refused. "Why should I waste my time making frittelle for these boys I've known all my life?" one of them explained to me later. For this woman and her friends, Carnival is an occasion to go to other towns and meet other young men. The festive nature of Carnival relaxes some of the boundaries which normally separate young men from young women in this society, and the dances organized on festive occasions serve as opportunities for socializing with the opposite sex. To put forth any kind of effort for local "boys" with whom one has grown up and who are not considered marriageable is, in the opinion of Bruna and her friends, a foolish waste.

❦❦

Types of Festivals in Sardinia

In Sardinian towns, not all year-cycle observances are considered true festas. Many observances lack the formal organizational structure that characterizes a festa or festival proper. There are three principal types of festas occurring within the year cycle in Sardinia: *festas mannas*, large festivals honoring patron saints; *festas longas*, or pilgrimage festivals; and *festas de komitatu*, saints' festivals celebrated by only a small committee of devoted followers. The festa manna in Sardinia resembles patronal festivals elsewhere in Italy and throughout the Catholic Mediterranean. Usually the town's largest celebration, it features secular events such as music, dancing, and fireworks, as well as the mass and liturgy in honor of the saint. As each town has a patron saint, each town celebrates a festa manna once a year, and some towns, such as Monteruju, have two. The Feast of the Assumption is the larger of Monteruju's patronal feasts.

Pilgrimage festivals, or festas longas (literally, long festivals), take place in small chapels located outside the town proper, sometimes many kilometers away. The celebrations typically last nine days, a period of prayer and observance known in the Catholic liturgy as a novena. Because of the length of the festivities and the distance of the chapels from the towns, many chapels have rough accommodations for the pilgrims known as *kumbessias*, and the celebrants live, eat, and sleep in these during the festive period. In Monteruju, Santa Maria di Runaghes is a festa longa, although the chapel is so close to the town that the faithful no longer spend the night there.

This type of festival is a typically Sardinian institution, with few known parallels on the continent (Gallini, 1971:30). Clara Gallini, who has done the most complete research to date on Sardinian pilgrimage festivals, has theorized that these rural festas, extended through time by the novena village, developed as a strategy to periodically break down the isolation existing between villages and between families in the same village in Sardinia (Gallini, 1971:31). The rural chapel exists in counterpoint to the town; while the town closes in upon itself and turns its back to nature, the rural chapel is immersed in the natural world where the agro-pastoral work of the villagers takes place. This opposition of town and fields, urban and rural, culture and nature is one of the basic principles of the Sardinian worldview. The rural chapel serves as a meeting point for these cultural oppositions, a place outside the pale of society where society's rules can be suspended and the community can exist as a community, without the usual animosities characteristic of small towns everywhere.

Festas de komitatu are smaller observances, celebrated only by a group of devoted followers who constitute a kind of religious fraternity. In Monteruju, the festas of San Sebastiano and Santa Lucia belong to this category. San Sebastiano is observed by a group of shepherds and Santa Lucia by a group of agricultural laborers who years ago made vows to honor these saints in exchange for special help or favors. The celebrations are held in the home of one of the committee members after the mass in the saint's honor and typically involve refreshments of cookies and wine. The committee member offering the refreshment keeps the saint's banner and regalia in his home until the following year, when he passes it on to another committee member. The members of these committees described their organizations as a kind of mutual aid society, fostering cooperation among members of the same occupational category as well as spiritually linking them in the service of a saint. Festas de komitatu do not, however, link the entire community together through reciprocity and obligation, as do the larger patronal and pilgrimage festivals.

Organizing the Festival

As in many Roman Catholic areas in the Mediterranean and Latin America (R. Smith, 1975; W. Smith, 1977; Aguilera, 1978; Brandes, 1988), festivals in Sardinia are organized and financed by the cargo system. In this system, a *komitatu* (committee) of about thirty members offers the festival to the patron saint and the community. The committee is in charge of all secular aspects of the organization of the festival, from collecting funds and financing the entertainments, to choosing and procuring the various performers, to actually setting up the stage, lights, and decorations that transform the church square into a festive space. Putting on a festival requires hard work, dedication, and organizational skills. Those who are appointed to the komitatu to perform this sacred labor are known in Monteruju as *oberaios* or *obrieri*—literally, "workers." Obrieri must also contribute monetarily to finance a festival. In large, wealthy towns, festivals are still financed almost completely with the contributions of the komitatu, whose members have the resources to sustain extensive monetary outlay. But in Monteruju and other small communities, the komitatu holds a *kirka* (search), a form of ritual begging in which contributions are solicited from each village household.[7]

In a pre-market economy, the cost-sharing system served as a vehicle for the redistribution of wealth within the community. Surplus agro-pastoral products donated to the komitatu were consumed in the ritual act of celebration, a generous negation of the everyday state of privation and want often experienced by the average family. During the festival, everyone shared in a temporary state of equality made possible by the redistribution of goods on which the festival was based. But the introduction of a consumer economy and the existence of government grants for the purposes of sponsoring traditional festivals have introduced new variables into the traditional balance the festival created.

At the head of the komitatu is the *primu* or *obriere maggiore* (*prima* if she is a woman). The primu or prima is the principal organizer of the festa and acts as final arbiter when there are disagreements between committee members during the meetings. The primu and the members of the komitatu are appointed by the previous year's committee. Being primu or prima is, according to one Monteruvian, "certainly a burden, not only a financial one but also in terms of time. But it's also a kind of honor, a recognition of esteem." The community recognizes in the primu not only a responsible individual with the skills necessary to organize a festival, but also a host to the entire community and a representative to the spiritual realm of the saint.

As a host, the primu and to a certain extent the rest of the komitatu are bound by the rules of hospitality governing social exchange in the village. The importance of hospitality in Mediterranean society has been emphasized almost to the point of stereotype by ethnographers (Herzfeld, 1987:77). Host-guest relations are nevertheless one of the important venues of reciprocity and exchange in Sardinian society. As Herzfeld has argued, the role of host confers a certain power as well as a set of obligations (1987:79–80). By appointing an individual to head a festival committee, villagers are at once demonstrating their esteem and at the same time placing the individual in a position of *noblesse oblige*, giving the individual both the right and the obligation to host the community generously. Largesse on the part of the festival organizers is expected; if the entertainments are few and shabby, villagers will feel poorly hosted and express their displeasure by remarking on the *festa fea* (ugly or shabby festival).

The komitatu is also the arena in which the major changes in the festa are decided anew each year. The oberaios have the power to shape the festa to their specifications, introducing whatever innovations they believe will be well received. However, they must answer ultimately to the rest of the community, which may accept or reject the innovations that have been made.

Selection of the Komitatu in Monteruju

Because of Monteruju's small size, nearly everyone in the community serves at one time or another as oberaio for one of the three major festivals. Unlike in other towns, oberaios are not limited to three or four prominent families.[8] In fact, members of the town's wealthiest families are not usually selected as oberaios, as they reside elsewhere. However, other criteria are applied in the process of choosing the komitatu.

While the committees for the Assumption and St. Martin were tradition-ally composed of males between the ages of twenty and fifty, since 1983 women have also been included in both committees. A number of reasons were given for this change. The most frequently mentioned was simply Monteruju's small size and the lack of available participants from which to draw. Since a number of women are now employed and earning an income, it was felt that they, too, should contribute to the financing of the Assumption. Pasquale Pala, primu in 1983, explains:

> For the first time they put some women [on the committee]. Because before, this festival was under the care of men only. So we had to scare up some money—because each individual brings a quota of money; so they thought to put on some women as well, so there could be more money. Also because this town is so small, when they do these two festivals, either you're on one year, or you're on the next.

Another factor in this decision may have been the inclusion of men in the committee for Santa Maria di Runaghes since its revival in 1981. If a commit-tee which had previously consisted exclusively of women now included men, it seemed fair that the formerly all-male Assumption committee should include women. The inclusion of women on the Assumption and St. Martin committees seems to be an open recognition, in the ritual sphere, of women's growing economic power as independent individuals in the community. The primu for the Assumption, however, is always male, while the prima for Santa Maria is always female.

Oberaios for the Assumption may be either married or unmarried. How-ever, because the komitatu for Santa Maria di Runaghes is composed of only unmarried individuals, there has been a tendency recently to appoint married persons to the Assumption committee to avoid overtaxing the unmarried with too many festival expenses.

For the same reason, some care is taken not to appoint persons who have served on other festival committees within the same year, or who served on the Assumption committee the previous year. People from the same household are likewise not put on the committee together, for the quota is considered to be the contribution of the entire household rather than of the individual oberaio. It is thought unfair to burden one household with two quotas.

Other important considerations involve the composition of the entire komitatu. The committee should have roughly equal numbers of men and women and should be balanced in age: not too many young people, but not all older people. The personalities of the various members should not conflict excessively, hence feuding individuals or rivals are seldom put on a committee together. This is done to insure a committee that is representative of the entire community, so the resulting festival will, at least in theory, contain activities and entertainments which appeal to all the various age and gender groups.

Selecting the Primu

Because the primu bears so much of the responsibility for the organization and administration of the festival, the choice of this individual is much more serious than the almost casual choice of the other oberaios. The primu for the Assumption is always male, usually over thirty, and married. Of course, the primu must also satisfy all the criteria specified earlier for the oberaios. But above and beyond that, the primu must be someone who *se ne intende* (understands these things) and *ci tiene alle feste* (cares about festivals). The first phrase, "se ne intende," refers to the primu's abilities to deal with bureaucratic red tape and Byzantine administrative hierarchies in order to organize the festival. Leonardo Piras explains:

> So what it is, in Monteruju, you have to request from the SIAE [copy-right group] and pay the fees; you have to fill out all kinds of forms: "Uti-lization of Public Security," "Record of Stage-Testing" for the folkloristic dances and dialect singers and so on, these groups, these rock groups— "eardrum-busters," that's what I call them! And practically the president [primu] gets elected by the outgoing committee. That is, the primu acts as a president. So usually you elect the usual visible person who has the pos-sibility to get through this bureaucratic red tape. So they appoint me pretty often. For this reason I've been [elected] various times.

In addition to skill and familiarity in dealing with bureaucracy, the primu should also have a number of political contacts and be a capable grant writer. These skills are necessary in order to obtain the requisite governmental allow-ances for folk festivals. Pasquale Pala, a teacher, musician, and seasoned grantsman, explains:

> They have funds set aside—the president of the state, the president of the province, the prefecture and the ministry of the interior have funds ear-marked for these social things. . . . So I wrote three or four letters; and this guy answered me: "My dear Pala—" Dear, my eye! Anyway, he sent me 100,000 lire . . . and the president of the Banco di Sardegna sent me the same, 100,000 lire, because I knew his wife. Then I had written a lot of stuff about how it was the festival of the émigrés; I gave them a whole tearful spiel. . . . The strong point was the organization of an evening of boxing. Usually a boxing encounter costs about 10 or 15 million lire; but we didn't spend even one lira! Because the boxing matches that were sup-posed to take place in Cagliari, in Sassari were rescheduled to take place in Monteruju. All through contacts and friends, of course.

Thus, the person chosen to be primu or prima must be the type of person who has both the administrative experience and the personal contacts to facilitate obtaining funds and entertainments. This practically excludes anyone without some education and status within the community. Persons whose work has taken them outside the village are especially favored, as they are likely to have more helpful contacts.

These criteria for the position of obriere maggiore are of fairly recent introduction. Before the organization of the festival became formalized, requiring applications to the state for funds, dealings with agents for the musical entertainers, and other bureaucratic procedures, the primu had to be wealthy enough to foot many of the incidental expenses of the festival. For example, the musical entertainers and oral poets, who often came from other towns, had to be put up for the night and feasted. A poor family would not have the means to incur this expense, so the burden fell to the wealthier landholders.

The phrase *ci tiene alle feste*, as applied to candidates for the position of primu, is a bit more elusive than the simple ability to manipulate resources and people. Its overt meaning is "he/she cares about festivals." On the surface, it seems to imply that festivals are more important to certain individuals than to others, and indeed, this is the case. A few persons I interviewed did not care for festivals at all. Others liked the entertainments well enough but did not participate in any of the organizational aspects. The identities of these individuals are well known in the community, and clearly they are not nominated to the position of obriere maggiore. But the meaning of the phrase "ci tiene alle feste" goes beyond this, too. The individual who "cares about festivals" to the extent of being willing to put the time and effort into the role of primu is making a statement to his fellow community members that he is economically and socially able to shoulder the burden accompanying the role. To people from families which were once at the bottom of the economic pyramid but have now attained economic well-being, this can be a powerful and appealing prospect. It is among this group of persons who "care about festivals" that those most willing to take on the role of primu are often found.

The committee may choose to assign the role of primu for other reasons, as well. The appointment may function as an acknowledgement of membership in the community, or of a newly acquired status. It is not uncommon, for example, for a newly married man to be given the post of obriere maggiore. Elena Tanca explained:

> They usually try to reconcile these characteristics that the primu should have with happenings or circumstances that have taken place during the course of the year. For example, one who got married this year, has set up a family and is independent. If, in addition to this fact, he is a capable person, who knows how to organize the festival and so on, they take the opportunity and make him primo obriere.

In this case, the position may be likened to a kind of rite of passage by which the individual is formally recognized by the community as an independent adult member. In other cases, persons who have married into Monteruju and have become well-integrated into the social fabric, or émigrés who have returned after a long absence, may be given the role of primu at the next festival. Both categories of individuals need to be formally integrated into the community and the role of obriere maggiore allows this to occur within the ritual sphere of the year cycle.

The role of primu functions as an integrative device because it duplicates patterns of exchange inherent in the social relationships in the community. As head of the komitatu, the primu acts as a host, offering the festa to the entire community, who are his symbolic guests. The other community members then become his debtors; they "owe" him something in exchange. Since this pattern of reciprocity underlies nearly all social relationships in the village, by engaging in it on a public, symbolic level, the primu assures himself open recognition of community membership.

The Role of Primu and Political Power

The role of primu is essentially one of ritual power, but in Monteruju ritual power and political power operate according to similar principles. Both elected officials and members of festival committees are seen as having important reciprocal relations with the community. Both charges involve serving the public or producing for the public good; both also require administrative skill and qualities such as trustworthiness in the management of funds. Thus, both positions involve responsibility towards the community in return for election or appointment.

A number of examples illustrate the connection between political office and the charge of primu or prima. Individuals elected to the town council or the office of mayor are often put at the head of a committee in recognition of their achievement. In 1989, Monteruju's first woman mayor was appointed prima for Santa Maria di Runaghes. The prima who appointed her explained: "It is the first time in Monteruju's history that we can have the mayor prima at Santa Maria!" It was the first occurrence of its kind because Monteruju had its first woman mayor, and only women can head the Santa Maria committee.

But previous mayors had been appointed to head a festival committee the year following their election as well. In other instances, elected officials are appointed to this office for frankly political motives. In 1985, the komitatu clearly acted according to these tenets when it appointed the town's vice-mayor as prima for 1986. The city had just received a government grant for the purpose of urban renewal. One of the projects on the agenda was the construction of a square in front of the chapel of Santa Maria to facilitate the circle dancing during the festa. The appointment of the vice-mayor to the head of the komitatu was engineered to guarantee the completion of the project in time for the festa.

The successful organization and administration of a festival can also draw attention to an individual's potential as a politician. The relationship between political power and ritual power is explored fully in later chapters.

Attitudes towards the Role of Primu

Although the assignment of this role may function in certain cases as an integrative rite and a public acceptance of an individual's place in the community, most people are not pleased to head a festival committee. The position is no longer viewed as sacred work, or an honor to be undertaken, but as an imposition on leisure time. Scholars have tied these changes in attitude to the introduction of a consumer economy. In Latin America, an area which acquired the cargo system of festival organization from centuries of Spanish domination, Waldemar Smith (1977:148–159) noted that individuals preferred to save their money to finance their children's education or expand their businesses rather than spending it on the festival. Stanley Brandes (1988:54) noted that his Mexican informants preferred to spend lavishly on life-cycle rites such as weddings and baptisms, where individuals are readily recognized as the financial providers. Monteruvians expressed similar feelings and attitudes.

Moreover, as more people engage in wage labor, leisure time itself becomes a precious commodity. Rita, a secretary, explained: "Sunday is the only day I can go to the beach; why should I spend it going around doing the kirka? That's why I don't like being on these things." However, the charge of primu/a is nearly impossible to refuse. In one case in 1989, the designated primu actually resigned from the committee as his first official act, but this elicited widespread public disapproval (cf. Brandes, 1988:49). The only cases in which it is admissible to turn down the office are grave illness or a death in the family—occurrences that exempt individuals from the obligations of any form of hospitality.

The task of primu is rendered more difficult by the reluctance of the rest of the committee to shoulder a part of the burden. Leonardo Piras told me:

> Lately, the last few times, I felt like throwing up my arms . . . because of this type of couldn't-care-less attitude on the part of the committee. Because, here's what happened. Three years ago . . . there were 36 of us [on the committee] and four of us organized the festa. Four of us organized the festa! I don't understand this kind of I-don't-give-a-damn attitude. . . . I always say, let's divide up the tasks. . . . When you are president of these committees, you feel duty-bound to stick your neck out. This should require everybody's cooperation. Instead, when all the others start to wash their hands of it, then instead of going out Sunday afternoon, Sunday evening to do the kirka to organize this festa, you're busy from two months before every single Sunday, taking care of these things. Well then—just two years ago, when I was president, I said, "Well, the next time they make me president of one of these committees, I, too, will go to the first meeting, give my offering, and wash my hands of the whole thing!"

As the bureaucratic responsibilities of the office increase and the willingness of other committee members to sacrifice time for the festa decreases, the position of primu is perceived less as an honor and more as burden to be avoided at all costs. With the pool of available candidates as small as it is, it is not surprising that Leonardo and others who have been obriere maggiore several times tire of the task.

Because of the onerous nature of the role, in some cases, the naming of someone to the post of primu can be done almost as a vengeful prank. Elena described to me the following circumstance:

> If you suspect that a group put you on, like, "Wait 'til I fix you! I'll make you organize the festival!" Like if you're a lazy bum who always tries to weasel out of responsibilities, they say, "Well—." So the next year you try to get them back; next time you put on someone from the group who singled you out. You can have like a repartee, you know?

ᚳᚹ
Financing the Festival

The festa is financed through two main sources of revenue: *sa quota*, or the contribution of each committee member; and *sa kirka*, a form of ritual begging in which the committee members solicit contributions from each household in the village.

Sa Quota

Each oberaio must contribute a fixed sum (quota) towards the festival; this amount of money is usually determined jointly by the committee in the initial meeting. In 1986, the quota was 60,000 lire, or about $80. While this is a substantial amount of money, most households from which the oberaios are drawn can afford this contribution. This automatically excludes from the role of oberaio those who are living on very low incomes or are unemployed. However, the quota is thought to be the contribution of an entire household; thus an unemployed son, for instance, would collect money from his parents or others in his household for the quota. Virtually any householder with an income is likely to get drafted as oberaio for the Assumption at some time in his life.

Before the mid-1950s, when grain cultivation was dwindling and currency began to be widely available, the quota consisted of quantities of wheat. Each oberaio gave one *korbula* (roughly one bushel) of wheat towards the festival.[9] The wheat was then sold, and the money resulting from this sale was put towards the festival expenses. At this time, the oberaios were all male agriculturalists in the peak of their productive years, roughly between the ages of twenty and sixty. Because in Monteruju it was traditionally the males who did all of the agricultural labor, it was entirely fitting that they constitute the committee for what was then primarily a harvest festival. Each would draw from the fruits of his agricultural labor to give to the Assunta what was considered her due. Because wheat was usually plentiful in this period after the harvest, there was no great hardship involved in this donation.

Of course, salaries do not fluctuate according to the year cycle in the same manner as wheat, and now that agriculture is no longer the primary occupation, the whole idea of propitiation and thanks for a bountiful harvest is meaningless in the new economic context. This leads to some resentment on the part of committee members when it comes to contributing to the festival a portion of their income that they often feel would be better spent on a new car, a vacation, or some other consumer product for their own personal use. Nevertheless, it is nearly impossible for an oberaio to avoid paying the quota, since the primu keeps written accounts of everybody's contribution. Many conflicts thus center on the determination of the amount of the quota.

The amount of the quota is determined each year by the komitatu in the first meeting before the festival. Often this is months ahead of time, as early as January, to give the primu time to apply to the region for additional funds. Since the amount of funds needed depends to some extent on the amount raised through the quota, determining its amount is usually the first order of business. This first meeting is attended by nearly everyone on the committee, as all want to have a say in the amount of money they will have to spend.

The primu generally has some idea of the amount of the previous year's quota, either from written records or directly from the former primu. He makes this amount known to the committee members, and a lively discussion ensues on whether the amount should remain the same or be raised. Because of inflation, the trend in recent years has been to raise the quota slightly each year. Once the amount has been decided, even the dissenters pay up promptly.

Sa Kirka

The amount amassed from the collection of all the quotas is never enough to pay for the festival. Therefore, each household in the village must contribute an additional sum towards the expenses. The komitatu collects this through a form of ritual begging known as *sa kirka* (literally, "the search"). This takes place several weeks before the festa, usually on a Sunday afternoon. A group of four to ten oberaios, headed by the primu, begins to make the rounds of the village in the early evening, when the summer heat has dissipated and the town is beginning to come to life again after the torpor of the afternoon hours. Following no special route, the group moves through the streets, knocking at each door in turn. When the door is opened, the primu will usually say, *"Noi semus sos oberaios de mesaustu. Nudda mi dasa?"* (We are the oberaios for the Assumption [or Santa Maria]. Won't you give me anything?).[10]

A number of responses to the request are possible. The householder may immediately assent, retrieve the cash, and give it to the primu. More often, a kind of negotiation takes place; the householder will ask with some reluctance, *"Kantu keres?"* (How much do you want?). The primu may answer by stating the amount most families are contributing, or by indicating that any contribution is acceptable. The householder then contributes some money. If the cash is not immediately available, the householder may agree to take it to some neighbor who is on the komitatu at a later date. Some families choose to pay in installments over a period of several weeks; others, especially those on retirement incomes, may tell the committee to return at the beginning of the next month, or whenever the government pension is due. For this reason, the kirka is seldom completed in an evening but instead usually stretches out over a period of several weekends. Either the primu himself or someone he designates keeps a written record of each family's contributions. As the komitatu leaves the house, some householders call out, *"Fake sa bella festa!"* (Make it a good festa!).

As with the quota, contributions to the kirka were once paid in units of wheat or other produce. The donation of grain and other products crucial in the agro-pastoral economy to the festival committee, and the sale of that produce to obtain a festival of thanks and propitiation to the saint, served as a vehicle of redistribution of wealth in the community. The kirka was characterized by balanced reciprocity: produce was given to the Madonna in exchange for the promise of a good harvest the following year. The komitatu acted as the mediator of the exchange. Moreover, the exchange was based on the model of ideal reciprocity functioning within the community. The unwritten rules of this model were nevertheless clear: any action, gift, or exchange from one party to another must be reciprocated to maintain the balance.

Balance and Reciprocity in the Festival

Because festas are so clearly based on a model of reciprocity and exchange, and because the danger of imbalance is always present, there is often a feeling of quasi-paranoia among the oberaios of any given committee that townspeople are not contributing their fair share to finance the festival. There are endless discussions—for instance, about whether donations were more generous when wheat was collected, or now that cash is the medium of exchange—but the general feeling is that "people try to cheat you." Rather than creating a situation in which the status of the oberaios inspires townspeople to give more in order to appear wealthier (Tedeschi, 1980:89), exactly the opposite occurs: many oberaios claim that people try to find excuses to give less. Whether this truly is the case is actually irrelevant; what matters is the constant preoccupation that the relationship symbolized in the festival will not balance out, that people will somehow take advantage of the fact that everyone is supposed to contribute to the festa by trying to get something for nothing.

This is why there is a tendency to "punish" those who have not contributed to the festival by placing them on the following year's committee. The idea is that balance will be restored because they will have to contribute a quota, which is usually much higher than a family's kirka offering. Leonardo Piras recounted an example of arguments breaking out over this issue in the middle of a festival one night. During a musical performance, one of the oberaios, emboldened by drink, suddenly grabbed the microphone away from the musicians and began to shout that certain people on the square had no right to be there at all because they had not contributed to the festa. He specifically named several men present. Leonardo, himself an obriere that year, later went up to those men and offered them wine in an attempt to repair the damage done by his fellow committee member, after which he claimed they felt guilty and gave him an offering. The incident illustrates the lengths to which some will go to ensure that the balance of reciprocity is kept intact.

☜☞

The Festa System and the Consumer Economy

The introduction of a consumer economy and the shift away from an agricultural base have changed the balance that once governed the cargo system. No longer does the festival redistribute goods in the way it once did. Wage earning has also changed the value system of Monteruvians so that many see the display of consumer goods, the sponsorship of private celebrations, and the acquisition of an education or a larger business as surer markers of status than festival organization and financing. This has led to decreased interest in festival organization and increasing burdens on the primu or prima. The existence of government grants for the sponsorship of festivals has added another dimension to the process. Once a sizeable portion of the community's festival budget depends on such outside factors, the socioeconomic balance of the festival shifts from the ritual sphere into a purely political one. No longer is the primu a wealthy peasant who wishes to offer a festival to the saint (or a poor one who goes further into debt for the same honor); now he must also be a grantsman, a man (or woman) with political contacts outside the community, and an expert at unraveling bureaucratic red tape. These requirements put the office out of the reach of all but the middle class, a group which presently has little interest in traditional festivals as vehicles of devotion or entertainment. The results are evident in the growing reluctance of many individuals to head festival committees.

The other half of the problem stems from the changed expectations of festive entertainments, and the consumerization of folkloric forms such as the performances of *poetas* (oral poets) and *kantadores* (singers). The emergence of brokerage agencies to act as intermediaries between the performers and the purchasers of folklore is a phenomenon that has not been sufficiently documented by contemporary folklorists working in Sardinia and needs much further study. These agencies determine what constitutes folkloric material, set a price for its performance, schedule tours for the performing groups, and market their "products" through weekly television programs and the sale of records and cassettes. The aesthetic standards for the judgement of folkloric performance are thus removed from the immediate control of the community and placed squarely in the hands of the dominant cultural group.

In addition, escalating costs and shrinking resources have contributed to the reduction of the number of festivals each town can celebrate. A small community like Monteruju finds itself increasingly squeezed out of the market for these folklorized forms of entertainment. These problems are compounded by increasing mobility, which has transformed any public event such as a festival into a display event for out-of-town tourists. This has resulted in the increasing concentration of resources on a single festival as a source of tourist revenue and a vehicle of display. But due to growing inflation, this system is in danger of pricing even a modest festival out of the reach of a small community like Monteruju.

Notes

[1] Mannhardt's findings were re-researched in the 1960s by German folklorist Ingeborg Weber-Kellerman (1963, 1965). While the works of Mannhardt and his followers have clearly been superseded in the study of folkloristics, their ideas continue to be popular among many educated tradition bearers. Many educated Sardinians believe, for instance, that certain Carnival figures are in fact fertility symbols, that many feast days originated as pagan fertility rites, and so on. One woman made light of this with reference to a friend who was prima for Santa Maria di Runaghes: "By being on the committee, Elena is guaranteeing her future fertility!" she joked. The German folklorist Hans Moser has termed this process *Rücklauf* (literally, "flowing back"). For a full discussion of this, see Moser (1964).

[2] Robert J. Smith (1975:31) argues to the contrary that the *fiesta* of the Virgen de la Puerta in Outzco, Peru is celebrated not during a time of leisure, but during one of the busiest times in the year cycle.

[3] For an overview of the Italian year cycle, see Toschi (1959) and Cardini (1988).

[4] The custom of ritual begging at the Epiphany was briefly revived in January 1988. ET wrote: "As I write this [January 5, 1988, 22:20], I hear the strains of an ancient tradition, out of fashion these last years but now revived, perhaps in an ironic vein. . . . Tonight Franco, Bruna's brother, GF and someone else, I don't remember who now, are acting the part of the three kings. They are wearing white sheets and are on a donkey. PC, A's nephew, heads the group with a staff and a saddlebag. To tell the truth, I don't know whether the costume is traditional or simply an improvisation."

[5] While the papal ban abolished the rites and rituals of the religious fraternities in Monteruju, they have continued in other parts of Sardinia despite the prohibition. The best-known of these is the Catalan-speaking region of Alghero. For a full description of these customs, see Satta (1982b).

[6] Although Constantine is no longer officially recognized as a saint by the Roman Catholic church, his feast day continues to be celebrated and masses are said in his honor in Sedilo, Pozzomaggiore, and a number of other Sardinian towns.

[7] Brandes (1988) and Smith (1977) have argued that this system of cost sharing developed to alleviate the burden on the committee that is inherent in the cargo system. They see this development as essentially tied to the introduction of a market economy. In Sardinia, smaller towns such as Monteruju have had a cost-sharing system for at least 100 years, coinciding, perhaps, with Sardinia's integration into a larger united Italy.

[8] This differs from the situation in other nearby towns. In Thiesi and Pozzomaggiore, for instance, the primu bears a great part of the financial burden for the staging of the patronal festa. This sum can run into the tens of millions of lire. Therefore, only a few wealthy families control the organization of the festivals.

[9] William Henry Smyth gives the amount of a korbula as 750 cubic inches, or 1.75 gallons. Smyth estimates it took 5.5 square yards of "moderately good land" to produce this amount of wheat (Smyth, 1828:345).

[10] I was not able to find evidence of the use of a ritual rhyme for this occasion, either in the present or in past times. Ritual rhymes are used in other communities; see, for instance, Costa (1911) and Bottiglioni (1925).

Chapter 4

La Madonna Assunta
A Festival in Flux

Late morning, the Sunday after August 15, Monteruju's streets are empty.
Everyone is at mass in the parish church. The cars parked in the church square
and on the streets tell, through their license plates, the story of Monteruju's
economic and social trials during the last thirty years: they are from Como,
Torino, Genoa, Rome, and from Germany and Switzerland as well. With all
the returning émigrés and guests, the church is overflowing; the men spill out
onto the *piazza* while the children play under the stage, hanging upside down
from the metal beams. From the church the sound of the chorus rises; inside
it's hot, people are sweating; a woman wipes her brow with a handkerchief.
After mass, suddenly the streets are full again; everyone is out greeting and
embracing old friends. The air is heavy with the smell of roast suckling pig and
bay laurel, mixed with the tomato aroma of the sauce for the ravioli.

In the afternoon the streets will fill again, this time with people following
the procession; some reciting the rosary, some marching quite solemnly, others dragging in tow as they chat with friends. Slowly the procession will wend
its way through the whole town, passing in front of nearly every home, and
old women in mourning for who knows how many deaths will peek out from
behind the blinds for a second, only a second, to watch it go by.

By evening the piazza will again be filled, this time with young Monteruvians and kids from neighboring towns. Under the colored lights a rock band
will play; the noise is deafening and the elderly lock their doors and windows
against it despite the heat. A few are dancing, but most young people roam
the streets, where a tense, torrid atmosphere hangs: one couple is kissing
behind a staircase, while another walks hand in hand away from the village
on the main road, towards the fountain.

59

But in the bars and behind the closed blinds people are talking. The band is too noisy; why didn't they get a dance band? The singer practically did a striptease on the church square, her skirt was that short! And they didn't even play one traditional number, can you believe it? The obrieri sure gave us a lousy band. The one in another town was better. That was real fun; there was a famous rock star from the continent, people danced 'til the wee hours. Next year so-and-so is on the komitatu; I wonder what they'll do to entertain us.

🕸️

The Feast of the Assumption

It is the Feast of the Assumption of the Blessed Virgin in Monteruju. Monteruvians consider it to be their largest and most important festival. Along with St. Martin, the Blessed Virgin of the Assumption—the "Assunta," as she is called in both Italian and Sardo—is Monteruju's patron. In the Catholic liturgy, her feast day falls on August 15, but Monteruju celebrates this festival on the weekend immediately following August 15. The festa lasts three days: Saturday, Sunday, and Monday, with Sunday being the climax of the festivities. Monteruvians have several names for this festa; it is most commonly called s'Assunta or mesaustu, "mid-August."

But Monteruju's largest patronal festival is in trouble. The social and economic changes outlined in the previous chapter have upset the cultural system on which this festival depended for success and survival. A spreading consumer economy has introduced new forms of entertainment and new expectations into the mass of variables that combine to produce a festival; Monteruju, lacking the economic base of larger communities in the neighboring area, has found itself hard put to compete with them in festival size and showiness. As a result, many Monteruvians are losing interest in this festival, which has now become largely a spectacle for out-of-town visitors and returning émigrés.

In this chapter I outline the changes in this festival over the course of the last century, as well as the many complex factors that have led to the erosion of its unifying role; I also describe its celebration in 1986. Because so few written records are available to document the celebration of the festival in the past, I relied on oral historical accounts from living informants to reconstruct the old festival. One problem inherent in this approach is that what emerges from this composite of many memories is not the celebration of one particular festival but rather an idealized version of it located somewhere in the past. Past festivals also tend to be remembered for their glorious moments. Memory glosses over the disappointments and dissatisfaction, the in-fighting, and the disagreements that must also have occurred, and a devolutionary perspective is almost inevitable. The idealized concept of the festival preserved in informants' memories is nevertheless valuable to the ethnographer, because from it one can gain a sense of why the current festa is perceived by so many to be unsatisfactory.

Catholic and Sardinian Tradition

The Feast of the Assumption has a long history as a holiday within the Catholic tradition. It commemorates the assumption of Mary, the mother of Jesus, into paradise upon her death. This feast day is celebrated worldwide in Catholic and Orthodox countries and is particularly popular in Italy and Spain.[1] The celebration seems to have begun in the sixth century in Syria and Palestine under the Byzantine Empire. Some scholars maintain that the cult of the Assumption of the Virgin was introduced to Sardinia through Byzantine influence during the reign of the Emperor Mauritius (582–602), who imposed the commemoration of the Assumption on the entire empire (Piras, 1961:28). But no historical documents dating the custom to the period of Byzantine domination survive. Satta (1982b:215) argues that it was probably introduced to Sardinia through Spanish influence during the years of Iberian rule.

It is likely, however, that the festival supplanted an earlier custom which took place around the same time. The Romans celebrated a feast for Ceres, the goddess of agriculture, immediately following the grain harvest—roughly the time of the Assumption. Such harvest celebrations are similar to agrarian harvest customs widespread throughout Europe, the purpose of which at one time was the invocation of magical powers to insure the storage of the harvested grain without spoilage (van Gennep, 1951:v, 2137). Many elements of these pre-Christian customs became connected with the Feast of the Assumption (Weiser, 1958:290).

Mid-August was also the time of the *feriae augustales*, holidays established by the Emperor Augustus. In the early medieval period, the Catholic Church took over these holidays and superimposed a Christian ideology on existing customs. But mid-August, or *Ferragosto* in Italian, has remained an important time in the Italian secular calendar. Offices and business establishments close for at least a weekend around Ferragosto; many close for a period of several weeks as workers go on vacation. This contributes to the holiday atmosphere surrounding this festa; because of its placement in the calendar year, many émigrés return to Monteruju for their annual vacations, which fall during this time. The festa thus becomes an occasion for homecomings and family reunions as well as religious celebration.

In Sardinia, the celebration of the Assumption as a major patronal festival is very widespread. In Meilogu alone, 6 out of 15 communities celebrate major festivals on or around August 15 (see table 4). Gallini (1971), in her survey of the province of Nuoro, found 15 communities with novenas occurring during August, while a recent commercial festival calendar lists 79 communities in the province of Nuoro alone having festivals between August 10 and August 20. The importance of this period in the agro-pastoral year cycle is a likely explanation for the prevalence of festivities in Sardinian towns at this time, especially since not all of them are specifically held in honor of the Assumption of the Virgin. This festa takes place almost exactly in the middle of the summer season, when there is a natural break in the agro-pastoral

Table 4
Towns of Meilogu and their Festivals

Banari
S. Lorenzo, August 9–11
Madonna di Cea, September 8

Bonnannaro
S. Giorgio, April 14
S. Barbara, August 15
Madonna di Monte Arana, September 8

Bonorva
S. Giovanni, June 24
S. Lucia, May 1

Borutta
S. Pietro, June 29
S. Maria Maddalena, July 22

Cheremule
S. Andrea, November 30
S. Antonio, June 13
S. Sebastiano, January 20

Cossoine
S. Chiara, August 11
S. Maria Iscalas, second Sunday in September

Giave
S. Cosimo, September 26

Mara
S. Giovanni, June 24

Monteruju
Madonna Assunta, first Sunday after August 15
S. Maria di Runaghes, September 8
S. Martino, November 11

Padria
S. Giulia, May 22
S. Antonio, October 20

Pozzomaggiore
S. Giorgio, April 23
S. Costantino, July 8
Madonna della Salute, September 28–30

Semestene
S. Nicola, second Sunday in August

Siligo
S. Vincenzo, last Sunday in August
S. Vittoria, December 23

Thiesi
Madonna di Seunis, September 8

Torralba
S. Antonio, second Sunday in November

cycle: the wheat has been harvested and the cheese-making season is over. In addition to being a period of relative inactivity, the recent completion of agricultural labor left, in the past, a surplus of goods in the economy which could be spent on the festival. Angioni (1974:244) attributes the wide diffusion of these August festas on the island to a combination of factors: the economic surplus, the natural period of rest in the agro-pastoral cycle, the predominance of good weather during this period, and the historically festive nature of this period. What we are dealing with, then, is not a custom unique to Monteruju but rather one typical of Sardinian communities as a whole.

The Legend

While it is impossible to pinpoint the exact date of the introduction of this cult and its accompanying festival to Monteruju, oral history and legend link it with the plague epidemics that devastated many Sardinian communities around the end of the sixteenth century. Leonardo Piras, a 50-year-old town clerk, gives the following explanation of the origins of the festa:

> It was a kind of thanksgiving to the Assunta, who is co-patron of Monteruju, to thank her for the harvest. Along with St. Martin, elected patron of Monteruju in 1626 after the big plague epidemic. Because before, it seems that Monteruju was divided into three small sections, and the ruins still exist—of St. Barbara, St. Sistus, St. Mary and St. Leonard, which we're now trying to restore. After this plague epidemic, they elected St. Martin and the Assunta, and built the present-day church, abandoning all the others.

This explanation places the origins of the Assumption in Monteruju during the period of Spanish domination, when Monteruju was rebuilt in its present location after being decimated by the plague during the late sixteenth century. This connection between the Assunta and the plague recalls the legendary origins of the same festival in Sassari (Costa, 1937:118).[2]

What is interesting about this account is Leonardo's insistence that holy patrons such as the Assunta were somehow *elected* by the community because they had done it a special service. Once again, this points out the close connection between Monteruvians' perceptions of patronal relations in both the sacred world and the political one. In a later conversation, for instance, Leonardo explained that he thought the P.S.I. deserved to win the mayoral seat because its leaders had long been helping many Monteruvians with their tax returns.

Reciprocal relations between individuals and the deity can also work the other way around, as in the *promessa*.[3] The promessa is a *quid pro quo* agreement between an individual and a saint: the individual promises the saint a devotional act (making a pilgrimage, for example) in return for a favor (e.g., improved health). However, the Assumption in Monteruju is not dominated by the promessa. Monteruvians, it seems, do not turn to the Madonna Assunta for many favors; this role currently belongs to Santa Maria di Runaghes (whose festa is covered in the next chapter).

Other legends connected with the Assunta link her with death, but not as a savior. "The Assunta wants nine stars in her crown," a reference to the iconography in which the Madonna Assunta is portrayed as the Queen of Heaven wearing a starry crown, is sometimes given this explanation: "[E]very year before the Assunta nine babies had to die, because the Assunta wants nine stars in her crown." The implication is that the Assunta calls innocent children to heaven to be the stars; she is directly responsible for their deaths. The old statue of the Assunta, which is no longer used in the procession because of its fragile condition, depicts a woman lying as if dead on a bier. This statue was once the object of great devotion. In the central isle of the church, before the main altar, a "bed" was erected for her, with steps going up to it on each side. On top of this high "bed" was placed the statue of the Madonna Assunta and after the mass on the second day of festivities, the people would file up the steps to kiss her feet in their little silver slippers. To this day the statue's feet are worn from centuries of this practice. At one time, this was characteristic of many towns which celebrated the Feast of the Assumption in Sardinia (Satta, 1982b:215). Eventually this practice was abolished by the Church itself with the reforms of Vatican II.

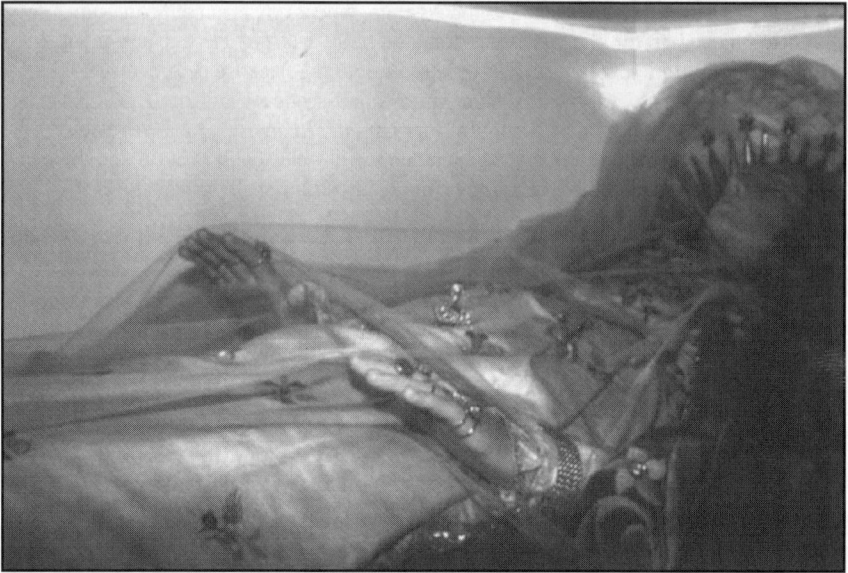

La Madonna Assunta

The modern statue which was ordered to replace the old Madonna in the bier is a plaster image with molded clothing. But the old statue was more like a large doll, which could be dressed. She wears a white dress embroidered with wheat sprigs and a blue mantle. This clothing was made for her by women of the wealthy families of Monteruju—as Satta notes, the wives of the prominent townsmen were usually the ones who were most involved with the care of religious matters, due in part to the fact that they had leisure time other women lacked (Satta, 1980:6). It was customary at one time for these women to dress the statue of the Madonna Assunta before the festival, and new clothing was made for her each year.

The symbolic representation of the Assunta as a sleeping or dead Madonna, her dress adorned with ripe wheat, points clearly to the chthonic associations of this deity, perhaps hearkening back to a pre-Christian feminine deity connected with the harvest and "death" of the grain crop.

❧❧

The Form and Program Structure of the Festival

Most patronal festivals in Sardinia share the same basic form and structure. As Smith (1975:9) explains,

> . . . each year's festival is novel though its structure remains the same. . . . Festivals exist in variations, in versions. . . . [T]he relatively fixed structure gives needed predictability; change in content and style gives novelty.

So, while each year's festivities give the impression of spontaneity and improvisation, this is only possible because each of the planners and participants share a common sense of the festa's ideal structure. It is the task of the planning committee to "fill in the slots," as it were, to create each year's festa anew.

The underlying plan of the festa follows a precise schedule, which varies a little from year to year but in fact is quite similar to the plans of patronal festas in other towns. Larger, richer towns may have more entertainments each night by scheduling two or more events simultaneously, but the general plan remains much the same. Because of Monteruju's small size and dwindling resources, its festa has what is considered to be the "bare bones" of what is necessary for a festival, and its structure is readily discernible. The plan may best be expressed in the timetable shown in the box.

Festa Timetable

Day 1 (Saturday)	6:00 PM	Evening mass in honor of Assunta
	9:00 PM	Entertainment
Day 2 (Sunday)	11:00 AM	Mass in honor of Assunta
	6:00 PM	Procession
	10:00 PM	Dancing and musical entertainment
Day 3 (Monday)	4:00 PM	Sporting event or games
	10:00 PM	Entertainment

Thus, the festival consists of a combination of celebrative elements (public entertainments) and ritual elements (religious practices) in more-or-less alternating sequence. The festival is structured so the peak events, the religious procession and biggest evening of entertainment, fall in the middle; the festive action rises on the first day, peaks on the second, and slowly tapers off on the third day of celebration.[4] The program leaves some flexibility for the scheduling of sporting events and musical entertainers, since these come from outside the village, must be booked far in advance, and are usually quite busy during the time of mesaustu with the quantity of festivals on that date in the island. The three days of programming also allow enough time slots for various types of entertainments to satisfy the different age groups in the town. Within this framework, each year's organizing committee has a certain amount of freedom to choose the character of the entertainments. These account for the variation of festas from one year to the next.

In spite of the program's flexibility, certain features of the festa are absolutely "fundamental," as one informant put it, and must take place sometime during the three festival days. In the religious sphere, these include the masses and procession; in the secular sphere, music, dances, and entertainments. Each of these is examined in turn in the next sections.

The Sacred and the Secular

The Feast of the Assumption is made up of both sacred and secular activities. Often, these spheres of action appear at odds with each other in the context of a single celebration: festive behavior consists of both prayer and drunkenness, devotion and licentiousness. In view of this

> . . . apparent ambivalence in the festival, it is tempting to divide it analytically into sacred and secular activities. Yet, for the people, the fiesta is all one. There is a time . . . for devotions and a time for merrymaking. The participants are always aware that they are participating in the fiesta of their patron and that . . . she wants them to have a good time. (Smith, 1975:109)

But the people of Monteruju are themselves aware of the opposition between the sacred and the profane during the festival. Many feel a kind of sheepishness about it. One man in his 50s admitted:

> Well, let's say that I guess we have to admit it, even though it displeases me to say so; the religious aspect comes last. Because in the name of the Madonna, we burn up every year, we spend ten million [lire]. . . . But people think about having fun, drinking, you know, having a good time. But the name of the Madonna, when you think about it, has nothing to do with it.

Others perceive the festa strictly in devotional terms and reject the secular aspect completely. "I can't talk to you about the festa," a 60-year-old woman told me, "because I don't go. I don't approve of festas." This attitude is more prevalent among women than men and carries a certain amount of prestige. To understand why, it is necessary to examine the official Catholic perspective on festival, the relationship between women and the Church, and the position of women in traditional Sardinian society.

Gender and Devotion

The Catholic Church has traditionally regarded patronal festivals mainly as occasions of religious devotion. Historical records the world over are full of the exhortations of priests and bishops against the "profane" aspects of religious festivals—"profane" usually being all those aspects which do not fall under the aegis of liturgy. Like many religious authorities throughout the history of festivals in Europe, the current parish priest in Monteruju laments the lack of religious devotion on the part of his congregation: "We still have a little bit of spirituality," he said, "but it has certainly decreased. The men, especially, do not take the sacraments as much as they used to."

In Monteruju, as in many Mediterranean communities, men have traditionally avoided religious functions and the Church in general.[5] It was women who were the main audience for the priests' teachings, and women who absorbed the brunt of the Church's doctrine. "Women's subordinate position in Sardinian communities insured that they were the ones to receive a whole series of moral values (humility, resignation, respect for hierarchies, etc.) contained in the Catholic message" (Satta, 1980:23). By allying themselves with the Church, women could acquire "a role and status through the values of purity, holiness, etc." (ibid.). It is natural, therefore, that women who see themselves (or wish to be seen) as deeply religious and adhering closely to Church teachings should adopt the point of view of the Catholic Church in the matter of festas; that is, that they are purely devotional in purpose and that the other elements associated with them are "profane."

Religious attitudes and behavior during the festival, then, must be considered in light of everyday attitudes towards religion in the community. For women, the festival represents an irresolvable paradox: its religious veneer barely covers up the fact that people are enjoying themselves. In Sardinian society, it is practically forbidden for women to enjoy an occasion of diversion without any element of sacrifice (Gallini, 1971:160). It is logical, then, to find many women, especially those aged forty and older who grew up without exposure to the new ideology of emancipation introduced through the mass media, embracing attitudes like those cited above. It is likewise not surprising that the main participants in the liturgical and devotional aspects of the festa are women.

The Ritual

The Mass
There are two festival masses: one in the evening of the first day of festivities, the other on the morning of the second day. The evening mass is usually attended by older women or those in mourning, for whom going to the festival mass would be an improper show of gaiety. The mass on the second day is the best attended, drawing a large crowd that spills out of the church and onto the decorated church square. The church is packed with women, children, and even men, many of whom enter church only for this occasion and for Christmas. Fresh flowers adorn the altar, and the new plaster statue of the Assunta stands on a pedestal before the altar, surrounded by masses of gladioli and other summer blooms. It is customary for the organizing committee to recruit a priest from another town to deliver the homily on festival days. Usually he is recruited by members of the organizing committee, and often he is a friend or relative of a committee member.

The Procession
The procession takes place on the second day of the festival, after the mass but before the evening's entertainment begins. It is the festival's climax and crowning event; nearly every able-bodied person who is not in mourning participates. Traditionally, the statue of the Assunta was carried in procession lying down on her litter. The present statue, however, is in an upright position, and is mounted on a base with handles so she can be easily carried through the town. In contrast to other towns with religious processions, the selection of men to be the bearers of the statue is almost casual.[6] Those who

are interested simply repair to the church a quarter of an hour or so before the procession is scheduled to begin. Sometimes there are not enough interested parties, and the priest must then recruit volunteers from the crowd assembled outside the church. Some men, however, arrange to bear the statue year after year. This was the case of Nicola Sabba, a 30-year-old factory worker who now lives in Porto Torres. He told me he carried the statue each year "for devotion." "It's as if by carrying her once a year I could expiate all my other sins—not going to church very often and so on."

As the four bearers make their way out of the church and into the afternoon sunlight, the band, provided by the Region, begins to play a marching tune, and somehow the untidy crowd that had gathered outside the church begins to arrange itself into the characteristic order. The order of the various elements in processions varies little from one town to the next. In the front is the banner dedicated to the saint; in Monteruju this is now carried by children, though in the past one man undertook this task year after year. This is followed by the young girls dressed in local costumes. The next section, once made up of women from the various religious sororities, now consists of a group of middle-aged and older women, recruited by the parish priest to ensure that someone would walk before the statue reciting the

Banners such as this one (of la Madonna Assunta) grace the front of religious processions.

rosary, since most of the people walking in the procession are interested in chatting with friends and pay little attention to the devotions. Behind them walks an altar boy bearing a cross, followed by the president of the organizing committee, the primu. Finally comes the statue, borne by four men, surrounded by the parish priest and the guest preacher. The general population follows, with the adult males close upon the statue, followed by women, teenagers, and children.

While the atmosphere at the head of the procession is solemn and reverential, the tail end is lively and engaging; for many people, it is a social occasion as well. A number of visitors from other towns appear for the occasion, giving old friends and acquaintances a chance to chat and gossip. "That's the best thing about [the festa]," said Nina, a 29-year-old teacher, "running into all these people you haven't seen in ages!" The festival thus provides an opportunity to cement or renew social contacts with persons from other towns.[7]

Young girls in local costume participate in the procession on the Feast of the Assumption.

The route the procession is to take is always a mystery until the last minute in Monteruju, but this was not always so. At one time, before the expansion of the town into the newly built area, the route all religious processions followed was the same. Since about 1950, though, portions of the circuit have been subject to modification. Some of these were introduced by the priest; others were yearly improvisation based on whoever was carrying the banner at the head of the procession.

The first modifications in the route were introduced in the early 1950s, when emigration had so depleted the population of Monteruju that there was nobody living on Via La Pace (known locally as *Carrella de segus*, "the back street"). Therefore, people began to resent having to walk all the way there in the procession. Since many took a kind of shortcut anyway, on certain years the procession, too, took the shortcut, eliminating about 100 yards of Via La Pace. However, the last member of a religious fraternity was living at the bottom of Via La Pace, and he became upset when the procession did not pass his house. He tried to exert his influence to eliminate the shortcut. Each year, therefore, there was always some doubt as to the procession's exact route.

Around 1975, the two sections of road connecting Monteruju with the new development in the valley were paved for the first time (previously they had been gravel paths). As people began to build and move into the new area, those planning the route of the procession had to take the new neighborhood into consideration. Since this time, the procession's route through the new development—and its inclusion in the circuit at all—has been a matter of debate each year, and the cause of infinite variations in the circuit route.

Because the procession is supposed to ritually mark the boundaries of the village while carrying to everyone's territory the blessing of the Madonna, this endless confusion over routes may be interpreted as reflecting some perplexity the Monteruvians feel in regard to the exact extent of their boundaries. The route of the procession has been stable only in its instability since 1975; in fact, it began to manifest some changes as early as 1950, when the disintegration brought about by modernization was just beginning. The confusion over this ritual act corresponds to the confusion Monteruju has felt about its status as a community. The present-day uncertainty as to the "correct" route for the procession may be interpreted as a ritual expression of Monteruju's growing dependence on the outside world: no one is really sure where the community ends and the outside world begins.

The Celebration

With the diminishing importance of religious ritual in the face of increasing secularization of culture, the celebratory aspects of festival have acquired greater importance in recent years. Many young people, especially, perceive the festa mainly as an entertainment in an environment otherwise lacking in stimulation. "We're kind of sick of them, but for us, there are few alternatives," Nina Solinas explained. "They're a way for people to get together and do something other than work."

But here, too, there is dissatisfaction, as Nina's comment shows, as well as generational conflict in the choice and evaluation of entertainers. The entertainments connected with the festival are also the main attractions for the hundreds of visitors from nearby towns who pour into Monteruju during the three festival days. This factor makes them important in the image of itself Monteruju wishes to present to the outside world. The caliber of entertainment a town can afford becomes a measure of the town's social, economic, and political status. Therefore, the quality and choice of public entertainments is of great importance to Monteruvians.

While at one time participatory entertainments were the rule at festas, all categories of public entertainments have undergone a shift from the participatory to the spectacular. Monteruvians no longer dance much but instead watch folk dance groups or rock musicians perform on stage. Sack races, greased pole climbing, and other such competitions have given way to spectator sports such as boxing and bicycle races. Nearly all age and gender groups expressed some dissatisfaction with this state of affairs, yet it has been virtually impossible to eliminate them altogether. The reason for this is the Assumption's status as a tourist attraction for visitors from nearby towns. Homemade entertainments convey an aura lacking in sophistication and limited economic means, which effectively lower Monteruju's status in the eyes of visitors. Thus, commodified entertainments persist, even though they leave many unsatisfied.

Recent years have seen an attempt to introduce entertainments which draw the community together without draining the committee's budget. Outdoor films, community soccer matches, nature hikes on the mountain, and photo exhibitions provide many opportunities for participation and interaction on the local level. These activities appeal to all age groups, and they have successfully stimulated renewed interest in the festa, suggesting that some level of participation is necessary in the local aesthetic of the festival.

Music and Poetry

Music is an important part of the Festa of the Assumption. It may serve as spectacular entertainment in and of itself, provide an accompaniment for dancing, or call attention to the solemnity of ritual; but in each of these cases it marks the event as characteristic of festive time, apart from the ordinary and the quotidian.

At one time, one of the festival's main drawing cards was the appearance of either the *poetas* (improvisational oral poets) or the *kantadores* (singers). Cirese has called these "essential in both festive and daily life" in Sardinia (1963:85). The poetas belong to a tradition of extemporaneous poetry, which has been documented by scholars on the island since 1787 (Pillonca, 1982:149).[8] The traditional male singers, *tenores* (a cappella singers, not all tenors) or *kantadores a kiterra* (singers with a guitar), are another important

part of the festa's entertainments. These groups of three singers with a guitar-
ist sing traditional Sardinian songs: *mutos*, *muteddos*, and narrative songs in
the ballads tradition.

At one time, both the kantadores and the poetas were hired to perform
through the personal contacts of members of the organizing committee. Usually they performed for the price of a feast hosted by the primu and an hono-
rarium. Since the 1960s, however, this aspect of entertainment, like all the
other spectacles connected with the festa, has come to be managed by an
agency or brokerage firm. The agency acts as a middleman between the festival committees and the entertainers. It publishes slick brochures advertising
various performers in glorious terms, which it sends to all the towns on the
island. The committee then contacts a broker from the agency, who briefs
him on what groups are available and their asking price.

The introduction of this consumeristic aspect into the realm of traditional folklore has had a profound impact on the relationship between the
performers and their audiences. Economically, it had increased the cost of
hiring performers tremendously, so that a poor town cannot afford to bring in
the best performers. The largest agency on the island also has its own cable
television station, which broadcasts folkloristic programs featuring these very
same performers and markets cassette tapes of their performances. The standards of the agency largely determine which performers are accepted as "genuine" and which are not, setting the standard for folkloristic performances
throughout the island and often valuing one region's style over that of the others. Clearly, much further study is needed on the impact of this phenomenon
on the island's folklore.

Traditionally in Monteruju the tenores perform for the Assumption,
while the poetas perform at St. Martin in November. In other towns with a
single patronal festa, though, it is usual to find both performing at some time
during the festa. Both perform on a wooden stage constructed over a framework of metal pipe on the central square of the village, facing the church. The
audience for the poetas and the singers is much the same: it consists of mostly
older and middle-aged men. There are several reasons for this. The so-called
"golden age" of improvisational poetry in Sardinia occurred between 1937
and 1950 (Pillonca, 1982:154), a time in which men of these age groups
would have been in their youth. The poetry contest is associated for these
men with the festival experience, and so they seek to repeat this experience
when they attend a festa. Song and poetry is associated with the male occupation of shepherding in Sardinia—particularly the long periods of transhumance spent alone or in the company of other men watching sheep on the
mountainside. Even those who are not professional singers or poets engaged
in some form of oral extemporization, and many look at the festive events as
occasions to add material to their repertoire. But for those born after 1950,
the agro-pastoral life, with its emphasis on oral transmission, is a thing of the
past; thus the songs and contests have little affective value as emotional experiences. The language of the kantadores and poetas is highly formulaic, and

most young people, since they lack this personal exposure to the tradition, cannot understand it.

For émigrés returning home for the festa, however, the singers and improvisators have become symbols of the culture they left behind. At every festa one may find them perched near the stage's speakers, tape recorders in hand, poised to capture the sounds of the performance, familiar sounds they long for in their new environments. During the winter months, in fact, when island festas are rare, many groups of kantadores and poetas tour the continent, where they are invited to perform by Sardinian cultural groups in Germany, Switzerland, Belgium, and other European countries.

Persons under the age of 40 or so generally do not enjoy traditional entertainers. For many of them, the most attractive musical event is the performance of the rock band. While some other towns can afford to present well-known Italian rock musicians, Monteruju must usually make do with an inexpensive local band. To individuals who have been listening to Sting, Dire Straits, Bruce Springsteen, and Madonna—as well as Italian artists such as Zucchero and L'Ittifiba—on stereos and tape decks, however, these bands are a source of disappointment and embarrassment. Young people would like to be able to attract better-known rock stars to Monteruju, but the cost of this is beyond the town's means.

In Monteruju as in other towns, a marching band usually accompanies the procession carrying the statue of the Virgin around the town. These are groups of trained musicians provided by the Region on request for rural festivals. They dress in military-style uniforms and perform a variety of marching tunes from prearranged commercial sheet music. At one time, of course, there were no bands to lead the procession as it wound its way through the streets of the town. Instead, the procession was preceded by a fife player and a drummer.

Music is also part of the mass given on the second day of the festival in honor of the Virgin. For this *missa cantada* (sung mass), as it is called, a small choir of teenage girls sings a few religious hymns during the service, accompanied by the priest playing the organ. The girls in the choir attend weekly rehearsals, where they are taught new hymns by the priest. They practice for the Assumption, St. Martin, Christmas, and Easter services—the only times there is singing of hymns in church. Here, too, we see music acting as a marker of festive occasion.

Dance

Dancing has long been one of the most striking aspects of festive behavior to outside observers, and one of the most important to many participants. Three main types of dancing go on during the Assumption: the *ballo sardo* or *ballo tondo* (circle dancing); ordinary couples dancing, called *ballo civile* (civilian dance) to distinguish it from the ballo tondo; and rock dancing. All dancing takes place on the main square in town, directly in front of the church.

The ballo tondo or ballo sardo (literally, "Sardinian dance") is a circle dance in which men and women alternately join hands and move in a spiral pattern which winds in on itself, then unwinds.[9] There is nothing exclusively Sardinian about this type of dance, which is one of the oldest folk dance forms found throughout Europe; the name ballo sardo is of recent acquisition and was bestowed to distinguish this style of dancing from the couples dancing which was introduced after World War II. The ballo tondo has historically been an important part of festivals on the island. William Henry Smyth, writing in 1828, said:

> Dancing constitutes a prominent feature of all public festivities. . . . The most national is the *carola* or ballo tondo in which many people join hands, and make a monotonous circular movement. In Capo di Sopra [northern part of the island] it is danced to the voices of several men, who stand in the center, holding each other by the shoulders and singing in a peculiarly powerful and guttural tone. . . . (191)

By the early part of this century, the choir of male voices had been replaced by a single accordion player in many areas.

The ballo tondo is still considered indispensable to the festa, particularly by the older generation who retains the ability to perform it. "Monteruju has this particular," Pasquale Pala explained:

> No matter what kind of band comes to play, you have to always hire an accordion-player. Why? To play the ballo sardo. Because Monteruju has this tradition of the circle dance. Uncle Totoi, bless his soul, was an excellent dancer; he and his wife, I remember them. This man never missed an opportunity to dance. Another man who lived here across the street who died a few months ago, an old bachelor—he never left the house. He went out only on the day of the festa to dance the circle dance. That [the ballo sardo] is fundamental. They want it the same even now; but aside from the fact that there are no dancers—young people, that is, only make a mess—but earlier it was sacrosanct.

Recent years have, however, seen a growing disenchantment on the part of young people for this traditional form; "civilian" dancing had greater prestige than the circle dance because it belonged to the world beyond the village, a world idealized in films and magazines. Only now, when there are no young people in Monteruju who can dance the circle dance in the traditional style anymore, has the interest in relearning this genre been rekindled. But now the emphasis is on the ballo tondo as a way of preserving a culture which many feel has been lost, as Leonardo Piras acerbically put it:

> Since a few years ago . . . the young people started to protest when they'd play two or three "civilian" dances and then a ballo sardo; they'd start to protest. Then little by little, as we grew up and took the place of our parents, we started not to give a damn about circle dances. Now that I've arrived at this age—I'm 50 years old—I've realized that this is going against our way, our civilization, our way to express ourselves. In the past few years we have eliminated our own culture, with this Coke and whiskey and rock-and-roll. Got it?

Leonardo took particular delight in linking the disappearance of his way of life to American products such as whiskey and cola. Like many Sardinians, he perceives America as the source of much contemporary culture, and he never hesitated to point out to me, as a representative of the American hegemony, its deleterious effects.

Monteruju held a brief course in ballo sardo for the elementary schoolchildren during the time I was in the village. The teacher was a young man from Cheremule who headed a performing "folk" dance group. But the fact that the circle dancing has now become a subject taught in the context of school underlines its remoteness from the everyday lives of most younger townspeople; it has passed from the realm of folklore into folklorismus. In the Festa of the Assumption, the ballo tondo has become a symbol: it is now common for Monteruju and other towns to hire folkloristic dance groups to perform on one of the nights of the festa. No longer an integral part of the folklore within the festival, it has moved from the active, participatory sphere into that of entertainment and display.

It is not uncommon now for the ballo tondo to be completely absent from the Assunta. This is not to say that other forms of dance do not flourish during the festa. Couples dancing continues to be popular among the middle-aged individuals who grew up with it, and rock dancing is of course practiced by those 30 and younger, who do not know how to dance the couple dances. Rock dancing has the added advantage of not necessitating a partner; in fact, it is usually performed by groups of teenagers of the same gender.

Games and Sports

In addition to music and dance, games and sporting events constitute one of the main attractions of the festa, both for locals and for visitors from other towns. Of the festa in which he was the primu, Pasquale Pala said, "The strong point was the organization of an evening of boxing. . . . It was a huge success. That little square was filled to bursting. They had set up the ring in the middle, and there wasn't even room for a needle!" In recent times, there has been a marked shift from participatory games to spectator sports like boxing and bicycle races. The exact date of the change is difficult to pinpoint; nevertheless, most informants agreed that before the Second World War, most of the games at the festa had been of the homemade variety. Local youths would compete with each other in donkey races, sack races, and climbing a greased pole for prizes.

Presently, most sporting events which take place during the festival are brought in with the help of the Region. Petitions must be made to the appropriate government office months ahead of time for the booking of these events. The Region, in turn, uses these festive occasions to schedule meets for its junior-division athletes. None of the participants in the sporting events actually comes from Monteruju.

As in the case of dance and music, the increasing dependence on outsiders to provide entertainment that is then consumed, as a product might be, by other outsiders who attend the festival is evident. While the spectator sports are certainly more spectacular than local games, not everyone in the community is pleased with the change. Antonio Sechi, a 33-year-old military employee, told me, "They used to do nicer things. Those innocent, stupid games, whatever you want to call them: sack races, stuff like that. Well, I liked those things."

To consider the sporting events only as display would be in error, though. They also serve as occasions for all kinds of social activities. On the night of August 16, 1986, I observed a series of boxing matches held at Monteruju's soccer field. Of all the spectators, about 70 percent were men from nearly every age category. The rest were younger women (under 40) and children. A few bars had set up in trailers around the field, and people were drinking; a restaurant on wheels and a nougat vendor were doing a brisk business. The boxers themselves belonged to a regional junior division and consisted mostly of young teenage boys. But no one seemed to mind because few spectators actually focused their attentions on the happenings inside the ring. Instead, a number of other activities were going on: conversations with friends, especially friends visiting the festa from other towns; drinking; and "cruising" in search of members of the opposite sex. A large group of children played kick-the-can under the spotlights. The sporting event seemed to be only a backdrop for these activities, an excuse to be out on a warm summer night.

☙❧

Private Festivities

In addition to the public festivities described above, most people also engage in a great deal of private celebration with family and friends during the days of the festa. We have already seen how occasions of public spectacle such as musical events and sports serve as arenas for private social exchange between friends. But a large part of the festa experience is actually private in nature, celebrated in the home or among close friends. While some scholars have classified these activities in the broader category of "Popular Festivities" (Smith 1975:109), I prefer to separate them from the more public aspects of festival—those which are performed in the street or public square—because they differ from them in quality and effect. While most of the public entertainments discussed above fall under the general category of spectacle, and so must be organized or at least brought to town by the organizing committee, the private festivities which follow are celebrated by each person who attends the festival as an individual or member of a family group. They are not spectacular in nature; that is, they do not constitute forms of entertainment one can passively enjoy; rather, they require active participation. For many Monteruvians, they constitute the heart of the festival.

Eating

Eating, along with drinking (which is considered below), constitutes an important part of festive behavior. Most eating during the festival days is done within the home with family members. A few vendors still come to Monteruju to set up their food stalls from trailers parked off the main square; they sell sandwiches and soft drinks, nuts, beer and *torrone*, a sweet nougat associated with festivals. At one time there were many more of these vendors; they can still be seen in larger towns (with more lucrative festas) selling fresh-water fish and eels salted and grilled over an open flame. When the vendors still frequented Monteruju's festa, presumably more eating took place on the street outside the family context.

The central feast of the festival takes place on the second day, Sunday, after the mass but before the procession. The traditional foods associated with this day are *cicciones* (*gnocchi sardi* in Italian), very small dumpling-shaped pasta made with wheat flour, served with a rich meat and tomato sauce called *kizadu*. Kizadu differs from ordinary meat sauce in that chunks of beef are used instead of ground meat. An alternative first course is ravioli filled with ricotta cheese and parsley and served with a plain tomato sauce. The second course is almost always *porkeddu*, roast suckling piglet seasoned with bay laurel. Various vegetables and salads may accompany the meal, and the choice of dessert is likewise left up to the individual cook. But the two central dishes—the pasta and the piglet—are traditional elements which remain the same year after year. They embody, in comestible form, the chief products of an agrarian economy based on wheat cultivation combined with animal husbandry. At one time, the cicciones were all made at home by women a week or two before the festival. Today, although a few women continue this practice, it has become commonplace to purchase machine-made, packaged gnocchi sardi at the store. Informants claim, however, that the factory-made product is not as good as the homemade one: "They don't hold the sauce well," one informant said.

Most of the feasting is done within the family, and in fact this is one of the occasions during the year when family members who work or study elsewhere return home. This is one of the most meaningful aspects of the festival as it stands today, both for returning émigrés and for their relatives who have remained in the village. The large Sunday meal is the most typical time for family reunions, and it is considered important for all family members to be present. Laura Cossu, a 28-year-old student, told me how angry her mother was when she and her sister announced they were going to the beach on the day of the feast. "To her this is unthinkable, that I would not eat at home on the day of the festa," she said. But many young people share her attitude; Leonardo Piras said, "Maybe the day of the festa [my sons] go to the beach. Before, this would have been unthinkable!"

Not all young people have this attitude, though. Bruna Meloni, a 26-year-old librarian, told me she planned to return from her vacation in time for the festival because it is important to be home for the festival meal in her family: "I've never missed a meal at mesaustu in my life." On one of the three days of the festa, her godmother invites her to dinner; thus, the festa is an occasion to reaffirm parafamilial ties as well. The primu gives very large dinners on all three days of the festa for the band members, sports participants, and musical groups who have been invited to perform, in addition to his own family.

Drinking, of course, usually accompanies the feasting. While there are many toasts during the feast, this type of drinking is different in quality from the type occurring in bars outside the home environment.

Drinking

While formal eating is always a family activity during the festa, drinking usually involves friends and acquaintances. Drinking is for many people the single most attractive aspect of the festival; in fact, among men, drunkenness can become a permanent state during the three days of celebration. To my question, "What attracts you most when you go to the festa?", a group of men in their twenties responded, "The bottle!" A 21-year-old student added, "The bottle always attracts us. At festas, it's double rations!"

This type of drinking tends to center around the bars, both the single café in Monteruju and the trailer-bars which come to town for the occasion. Wine and beer are the most commonly consumed forms of alcohol. Although men of all ages are most apt to be found drinking in bars, a number of young women also participate in this activity. Drunkenness is rarely seen in women, however, and the bar tends to be more of a focal point for social encounters than a source of alcohol in and of itself. Nina was quite upset that the boxing match was located at the soccer field in 1986, rather than in the central square as had been previously done. "I don't know about these deluded obrieri who gave us this sewer of a festa!" she complained. "Half the fun of the festa is walking back and forth from the bar to the square." It was clearly not the drink that attracted Nina, since plenty was available at the boxing match from itinerant vendors. Rather, it was the bar as one important focus of activity during the festa (the other being the square). The central importance of the bar at this time was underlined by another informant, who said, "The bars are always fuller than the streets."

Courtship, Sex, and Licentiousness

Part of the reason for the attractiveness of bars to Nina and other unmarried women her age is the presence of large numbers of men, especially men from other towns. The meeting of members of the opposite sex is, to quote one 21-year-old male, "one of the main reasons you go to festas." "I go to meet women," Marco Mannu told me. "I started officially going with my girlfriend at a festa." In fact, I spoke with two married couples who claim to have met at festivals. Since, as we have seen, the dances no longer serve as meeting places for young men and women because people tend to dance to rock with others of their own sex, the bars have now taken over that function. They are one of the few settings in which young men and women can interact informally without the knowledge of their families—a knowledge which would bring with it greater social obligation and give the exchange an all-too-official air. While this type of behavior is encouraged in young men and tolerated in young women, once a woman marries it is expected to cease. One married woman who continued to frequent the bar with great regularity, both during the festival and at other times, was heavily criticized for this behavior, both by her husband (who publicly accused her of infidelity) and by the community at large.

Aside from the obvious importance of the festa as an occasion for courtship, it is nearly impossible to ascertain the amount of sex which takes place during the festival, as these activities are by nature kept private (cf. Smith, 1975:122). I did not see instances of open ribaldry and licentiousness, as might be seen at Carnival (Counihan, 1985); however, this does not mean they did not occur. It is likely that my status as a young unmarried woman with strong, quasi-kin connections in the community served to insulate me against this type of display, which would have been considered offensive and perhaps not in the best interests of the community itself as it wished to be perceived. Also, I did not engage in flirtatious behavior while at the bar, and thus possibly excluded from my study a certain type of data.

Dress

Dress is an important aspect of festive behavior, largely because so much of festival activity centers around seeing and being seen. Especially before outsiders who are unfamiliar with one's everyday persona, Monteruvians wish to put their best foot forward. Young unmarried people are those most concerned with clothing for the festa because of its potential in attracting the attentions of the opposite sex.

It is customary for children and young people to acquire new clothes for mesaustu. Often a special shopping trip to Sassari is planned for this purpose. Since many weddings and baptisms also occur during August, one new outfit is typically purchased to serve for all the festive occasions one is to attend. The types of clothes vary, of course, from individual to individual according to tastes, styles, and economic factors, but usually they represent a dressy version of normal street clothes. While men and women over thirty seldom indulge in the purchase of new outfits especially for the festa, there is a general agreement that on festival days one should dress "well." It is still common to see some older men in black wool suits and starched white shirts during the festa. Middle-aged and younger men do not wear suits, but some combination other than the functional work clothing they wear every day. Middle-aged women, who typically do all the cooking, cleaning, and household preparations, will change into their best clothes to attend the mass and walk in the procession; otherwise they wear housedresses that will not be spoiled by stains and spills.

At one time, festive dress consisted of what is called the *costume*, a kind of regional costume. For women, it consists of a narrowly pleated wool felt skirt, usually red; a white linen blouse; and an embroidered velvet corselet worn over the blouse and fastened with ornate silver filigree buttons. A black silk apron is worn over the skirt. The men's version consists of black wool trousers, a white linen shirt and black overvest, and black wool stocking cap. According to older informants, this was the festive dress of sixty to one hundred years ago; couples were married in the costume and wore it for other festive occasions throughout their lives. Presently, most families have in their possession at least a few elements of the costume. Since five or six years ago, it has become the fashion, in imitation of folkloric groups in other towns, for the children in Monteruju to dress in costume and parade in the procession. Usually only girls between ten and sixteen dress in this way; older women and boys consider it vaguely embarrassing.

Other Preparations

Every household undergoes a number of small, private preparations for the festa. At the very least, the whole house is given a thorough cleaning, clothes and bed linens are washed, rugs are aired, mattresses are taken apart and the wool in them changed. Those with front gardens or porches trim geraniums and sweep furiously to insure that their homes will give the best impression to visiting outsiders. Some people even wash their cars on the day before the festa, though they would hardly use them for three days. Monteruju's tiny general store bustles with clients as women hurry to buy up merchandise for the feast before it is all gone. Many women prepare food ahead of time for the festa and freeze or refrigerate it so they can work less during the festival days; this is obviously a recent development, as in the days before refrigeration food was to be immediately consumed.

The household preparations, much like the decoration of the town in the public arena, transform the ordinary living space into the festive, the sacred. Many of the acts of preparation involve cleaning—a purification, as it were, for the coming feast. When the festa arrives, everything must be transformed; nothing is allowed to be undone or in disorder. The festa itself will create disorder: dirty dishes, people coming in and out of the house, bringing in dust; but in the calm before the storm, the stage must be set for the consumption of the sacred.

The Feast of the Assumption in Monteruju is a festival in flux. No longer strictly tied to the economy, the introduction of a regional government office which disburses funds for local festivals has changed the economic mechanism according to which it once operated. The consumer economy has introduced costly new elements into the traditional festival plan which require large amounts of capital to acquire, or has inserted the profit model into old forms which could once be financed through exchange. This model has changed many of the participatory activities connected with the festival to spectator events. Different expectations of festival entertainment divide the generations, and the community lacks the financial base to satisfy all its members. At the same time, the values which once made the role of primu a coveted affirmation of status have disappeared, to be replaced by a higher valuation of leisure time and personal expendable income. The growing complexity of festival organization has made the position into a bureaucratic headache few wish to take upon themselves. All of these factors have contributed to a growing disenchantment with the festa on the part of nearly every age group. The festival continues to be observed because of its increasing value as a tourist attraction for visitors from nearby towns and for returning émigrés. For many Monteruvians the festival has important affective associations.

Notes

[1] The worship of the Virgin Mary as the mother of God was a relatively late development in Catholic history. It seems to have originated in the Middle East around the fourth century, though in this early period it received no official endorsement by Church authorities. The Council of Ephesus first legitimized the cult of Mary in 431 CE. From this time on, the cult spread and grew in popularity, gaining a strong foothold in the Mediterranean area. For an interesting and intriguing explanation of the popularity of the cult of the Virgin in Mediterranean countries, as well as a new interpretation of the reasons behind its late acceptance into Catholic doctrine, see Carroll (1986).

[2] In Sassari, an elaborate procession takes place each year on August 15 to expiate a promise made to the Assunta in 1580 in return for protection against the plague. According to legend, the inhabitants of Sassari were spared from the devastations of the plague because of this elaborate display in honor of the Virgin, their protectress (Costa, 1937:118). It is possible that this well-known legend, which is reprinted in local newspapers each year as the date approaches, has combined with the popular idea of the origins of the festival in Monteruju. It is also possible that the custom of a festa in honor of the Assumption was borrowed from Sassari by the Monteruvians in the seventeenth century.

[3] The promessa is a request made of the saint in exchange for devotion. Typically, when the desired outcome has been achieved, the devotee will buy an offering to give to the saint in memory of the "miracle" which has been done. These ex-votos may be paintings which depict the circumstances requiring the saint's intervention, gold or silver charms in the shape of the part of the body healed through divine aid, or silver medals simply inscribed "GR," *per grazia ricevuta* (in recognition of grace received).

[4] This is quite similar to the pattern Smith describes for the fiesta of the Virgen de la Puerta in Peru (Smith, 1975:137) and is in fact typical of most patronal festivals in the Catholic world.

[5] Gallini gives several reasons for this phenomenon. First, the strong peasant value on work and the economic necessity of agricultural labor did not often permit interruptions of the kind imposed by the official liturgy. Secondly, men had at one time (and continue to have, to some degree) more possibilities for social exchange outside the home than women. Men could frequent the bar, lounge openly in the street, and travel freely as migrant laborers—all occasions which permitted plenty of opportunities for socializing with other men. This greater freedom and exposure to the outside world allowed them to develop a more critical and detached attitude towards the Church and its representatives (Gallini, 1971:169).

[6] In some Italian towns, the posts of bearers of the saint's statue are auctioned to the highest bidder. See, for example, Tedeschi (1980).

[7] Many processions end with an eruption of firecrackers. While this was true in Monteruju until 30 years ago, it is no longer the case today. At one time, it was the custom to distribute among the oberaios some *nughe-bumbas*—literally, "nut-bombs"—which must have been similar to firecrackers or cherry-bombs. Each oberaio had a few, and the primu had more. As they

were marching, when they would pass the home of one of the committee members, the others would set off one of these firecrackers. This seems to have been a form of public acknowledgement of those being honored by serving on the organizing committee. It is not surprising the custom has vanished now that it is no longer a mark of particular esteem to serve on the committee, although other informants ascribed it to the dangerous quality of firecrackers.

[8] Numerous scholars have studied oral improvisational poetry in Sardinia. For an overview of the genre, see Pillonca (1982). Cirese (1963) has done the most comprehensive study of the form and structure of Sardinian oral poetry. For a discussion of the effects of mass media and consumerism on the performance of oral poetry, see Lortat-Jacob (1981):185–197.

[9] See Galanti (1950).

Chapter 5

Santa Maria di Runaghes
A Festival in Resurgence

Summer is already fading in Monteruju; you can feel it in the wind that blows in the evening as pilgrims make their way up to Santa Maria. They are going to the novena for the festival of Santa Maria di Runaghes. The old women go in droves; every evening a group of them swathed in black shawls crosses paths with a shepherd coming down with his flock—a black huddle meeting a white huddle. The night of the festa almost everyone goes up. There is a long line of cars outside the sanctuary; the air is rich with aromas—boiled mutton, onions, wild fennel, and mint. The smells persist during Mass, making mouths water. As the priest delivers the homily, the sun sets in the valley and the mountain, on the east, takes on a pinkish cast under the turquoise sky. The first stars come out, then the moon rises over the mountain, casting its light on the whole community. Tonight under that light they will dance the circle dance in Monteruju: a long serpentine that winds around and around on itself, pulling you with a force of its own, dragging in front of you friends and enemies, young people and old people, adding new characters until it becomes as long as life itself. From her pedestal Santa Maria watches it all with her blue glass baby-doll eyes—those eyes that seem to look right through you.

The festa of Nostra Segnora di Runaghes is celebrated in Monteruju on September 8. Although it occurs very near in time to the festa of the Assumption—in some years only two weeks afterwards—it is a very different type of festival. It is a festa longa, preceded by a novena and celebrated not in the patronal church inside the town, but at a small chapel located on a rise about half a kilometer (a quarter of a mile) from the town proper.[1] Because of the period of devotion preceding it, it has a more serious cast than the Assumption; many refer to it as a *festa religiosa* (religious festival).

Chapel of Santa Maria di Runaghes

The name of this church, Santa Maria di Runaghes, derives from a local form of the word *nuraghe*, a sort of prehistoric stone tower which dots the island (Wagner, 1960:II, 176). In fact, according to oral historical accounts, near the chapel there was once a nuraghe that was taken down when the present cemetery was built.[2]

There are various names which the Monteruvians use in referring to this festival. Most commonly, both the church and the festival are called "Santa Maria." The appellation *Nostra Segnora di Runaghes* is slightly more official and appears on the mimeographed version of the *gosos* (hymn) which is circulated during the festa.[3] *Nostra Segnora de Capidanni*, or Our Lady of the New Year, is another name for this festa, and refers to the timing of the festival (within the first week of the Sardinian new year). The festa—and indeed, the whole period of the year in which it occurs—is also commonly referred to in the plural form, *sas Marias*—literally, "the Maries." A satisfactory explanation for this remains to be found. Some people thought it might be because so many towns in the vicinity celebrate this date in honor of the Virgin (see table 4 in chapter 4).

In spite of the fact that many towns celebrate the Nativity of the Virgin on September 8, Santa Maria di Runaghes is felt by Monteruvians to be unique to Monteruju. In comparing her with the Assunta, they often say, "The Assunta is everywhere, but Santa Maria is special for Monteruju." This proprietary feeling towards this Virgin is accompanied by a particularly strong show of devotion towards her, manifested in ex-votos (gifts left in exchange for miraculous help, often commemorative) and reports of miraculous healings which have occurred as a result of her intercessions. For these reasons as well as for others, which are examined in detail below, I will argue that Santa Maria di Runaghes plays a pivotal role in the maintenance of Monteruju's sense of identity and distinctiveness vis-à-vis nearby communities.

Occurring as it does at the end of the summer, when the cheese-producing season is over and the sheep are beginning to breed, the festa of Santa Maria marks an important time of transition in the year cycle. According to van Gennep, such customs in pastoral societies serve to mark the return of sheep from the summer pastures in mountain towns, while in hill towns they are often the "prolonging or repetition of spring pastoral customs." Usually, this transition is symbolically represented by processions from low places to higher ground, or to chapels in out-of-the-way places (van Gennep, 1951:1/v, 2137). All of these generalizations apply to some extent to Monteruju's festa of Santa Maria di Runaghes. While Monteruju has no true transhumance, sheep are nevertheless taken to pastures on higher ground during the hot, dry summers, as there is greater likelihood of fresh fodder in higher locations. At the end of the cheese season, sheep are usually brought to pastures closer to the village for mating. At the same time, the festa may be seen as an echo of the May rite in which women pray each evening at the little chapel of Santa Maria, which is kept open for the entire month of May expressly for this purpose.

The fact that the chapel of Santa Maria is opened only during the month of May and during the days of the festa should underline the connection between these two rites. While the May rite may be seen as one of propitiation to insure the growth of plants that provide fodder for the sheep, the festa of Santa Maria in September closes the cycle, marking the end of another cheese-producing season and the beginning of a new agro-pastoral year. In the modern industrial and temporal year-cycle, this festival also marks a transition: it is the end of the summer holiday season, when workers return from their vacations and schools open again.

‿‿‿‿
History and Diffusion

The existence of a year-end festival at the beginning of September involving a pilgrimage to a chapel outside the town limits is certainly not unique in Sardinia. In fact, in the Meilogu region alone, an astonishing number of communities celebrate such festas on September 8 or thereabouts (see table 4 in chapter 4). Although this is the Feast of the Nativity of the Virgin in the Catholic Church, and all Catholic communities observe this occasion, the festas listed in table 4 as occurring on September 8 all involve pilgrimages to sites outside the towns themselves. Moreover, these communities are close together, suggesting either a common historical origin for this type of festa or diffusion from one original center. In addition, five out of eight communities with September festas also celebrate a major patronal festa shortly beforehand, usually in mid-August (see table 4). This combination of traits suggests that Monteruju's constellation is in fact typical of Sardinian towns in this area, which were characterized by mixed agro-pastoral economies.

September 8, in the Catholic liturgical calendar, is the Feast of the Nativity of the Virgin. Like the Assumption, this feast was introduced to the Catholic Church from the Orient during the seventh century. As the scriptures do not mention directly Mary's date of birth, the date is thought to be that of the dedication of a Marian church in Jerusalem. The celebration of this feast spread more slowly than that of the Assumption, but by the twelfth century it was observed in all Christian countries (Weiser, 1958:304). In many places, it coincided with the end of summer and the beginning of the fall planting season.

The exact date of the introduction of this feast to Sardinia is uncertain. Piras (1961:97) dates the similar festival of Santa Maria di Seunis, in nearby Thiesi, to the medieval period, which brought to the entire island a flowering of interest in Marian cults. If indeed the cult of the Madonna di Seunis dates from this period, it is not unlikely that Santa Maria di Runaghes, too, can be traced to the same time period. This fits well with the history of novenas in general, which became especially popular during the Middle Ages in connection with Marian worship.[4] However, pilgrimage festivals in their present form were probably a product of the Counterreformation, when Sardinia was under Spanish domination (Gallini, 1971:30–31).

The little chapel of Santa Maria cannot be dated to a specific time, though it was probably built around 1600 like much of present-day Monteruju. The original structure is apparently buried under successive layers of construction, and it is possible there may be additional structures on the site beneath the present one. The chapel stands near the remains of a nuraghe and a group of Neolithic shaft-tombs dug into a low hill. It is widely believed that the chapel, and the festa itself, are very ancient in origin. According to one oral historical account:

> Santa Maria di Runaghes was [once] the major festa; it was celebrated the 8th of September, like today, always at the end of the harvest. But it was replaced by the festa the Sunday following August 15th. Earlier they celebrated the Madonna di Runaghes; then they elected the Assunta co-patron.

The accuracy of this assertion cannot be ascertained but when the church was under restoration during the years between 1971 and 1979, various informants reported finding evidence of human remains while they were assisting with repairs. The bones were interpreted as belonging to those who had died of the plague during the sixteenth century. These finds quickly became assimilated into the considerable body of legend surrounding this chapel and Santa Maria di Runaghes herself, and they were taken as evidence of the ancient origins of the structure.

According to Gallini (1971:30), the probable origin of all rural festas is very old, perhaps pre-Roman. The foundation of a certain number of these rural chapels near nuraghi or other archeological remains can be traced to the influence of medieval monasticism, when the Catholic Church endeavored to pull into its fold the final vestiges of pre-Christian worship on the island. The symbolic associations of Santa Maria di Runaghes with rain and fertility (see below) and the location of her shrine next to a prehistoric ruin would lead us to believe it likely that her cult developed in medieval times on the site of the earlier shrine of a pre-Christian deity. However, there is not enough evidence to know what form, if any, the festa took before the beginning of the twentieth century.

The chapel of Santa Maria di Runaghes lacks the *kumbessias* (living accommodations) for pilgrims that characterize other rural chapels in Sardinia. At one time, according to oral historical accounts, it was customary for women to spend the night at the chapel during the novena, but there was never a true novena village to house pilgrims coming from faraway towns. Today the custom of spending the night at the chapel has disappeared; the village has grown so it is physically closer to the chapel, and the presence of cars has made it easy to travel to Santa Maria in a matter of minutes.

In other aspects, however, it is typical of Sardinian pilgrimage festivals. As the Festa of the Assumption becomes increasingly oriented towards tourists from nearby towns, and thus the world outside the community, and as Monteruju's independence as a village decreases, villagers long for some rallying point to provide them with a sense of community and identity. Since its revival the Festa of Santa Maria di Runaghes has become this rallying point. This has been accomplished through a combination of the actions of individual festival organizers and community reaction which have contributed to the shaping of this tradition. In this chapter, I examine the festa and the process through which it has acquired its present form.

The Legends

Both Santa Maria di Runaghes and the location of her chapel are the focus of a number of legends, beliefs, and magico-religious practices in Monteruju. While the Madonna Assunta is conspicuous for the scant legendary materials associated with her, all of the Monteruvians' hopes for miracles and speculations about the supernatural world seem to have clustered around the Madonna di Runaghes. It is to her that ex-votos are usually promised, that gifts of flowers, jewelry, and handicrafts are brought, and it is she to whom the devout turn in the face of real tragedy.

Linda Dégh has described the legend as

> . . . an unuttered question on man's microcosmos. . . . The legend explains an extraordinary phenomenon or a memorable event, it communicates traditional learning and knowledge to the young and the uninitiated, it advises people how to act in critical situations and warns them against doing the wrong thing. (1972:74)

The narratives collected about Santa Maria di Runaghes correspond closely to this description. For the most part, they may be considered religious legends, although many "pre-Christian beliefs infiltrated the stories about saints, martyrs, and miracles stimulated by the early Christian church" (ibid., 76).

The most widely reported legend concerning Santa Maria di Runaghes is associated with her extraordinary powers to cause rain during a drought, or to stop rain when there was too much of it. Angela Ragas, 87 years old, remembers:

> They would bring [the statue of Santa Maria di Runaghes] to Monteruju
> when there was either a drought, or too much water. Then they would go
> to the priest and say, "We want Santa Maria. . . . !" Before, they had this
> custom. And they would . . . say mass. Three days, and immediately the
> water would come! And if there was too much water, as soon as they
> opened the door [of the chapel] it would clear up immediately.

This practice was once widespread in Sardinia. As Atzori explains, "In
the past, during periods of drought, Sardinian agriculturalists put their last
hopes in forms of magical propitiation to obtain rain from the divinity"
(Atzori and Satta, 1980:115). The Sardinian custom of carrying saints' statues in procession and sometimes even dunking them in a drinking trough to
bring about much-needed rain has been documented by Costa (1911), Bottiglioni (1925), and Alziator (1978). The practice is, of course, not limited to
Sardinia but found also in other Catholic areas.[5] In Sardinia, however, the
problem of drought has always been the biggest menace of both agriculture
and pastoralism, and thus it has become a particular focus of folk religious
practice (Atzori and Satta, 1980:115–116).

In the following legend, collected from a number of informants but narrated here by 67-year-old Pietra Angela Cossu, the connection between Santa
Maria and rain is emphasized by the violent storm that prevents the devout
woman from returning home to her family. Because of her devotion, the
Madonna sees that her family is not neglected while she is at her prayers:

> This woman, they say her husband had beaten her. He used to beat her.
> And she went all the time to Santa Maria. One day it was raining; she
> couldn't come down. But she was worried for her children. And also for
> her husband, of course. But she could not go down just the same. In the
> morning she went down; and it was as if she had been there herself. But
> instead they say she could not move. And Nostra Segnora went there in
> her stead. She was full of virtue, eh? This old woman, this was four cen-
> turies ago. She was a holy one, always praying. And then they said that
> then at night Nostra Segnora went down to her house. But she continued
> all night. She spent the whole night praying, and in the morning she went
> down. She goes down; and she meets her husband. "Last night," she
> said, "last night—" "You were here!" [6]

Other legends involve the location of the chapel of Santa Maria, which is
variously said to have been the site of the dance of the dead and the hiding
place of buried treasure. The following story was told to me by Luisa Cossu,
a schoolteacher from Monteruju who once studied folklore at the University
of Cagliari, but she recalled this tale from her early childhood.

> The dead did the circle dance in the porch at Santa Maria like when they
> were alive. And [my brother] told about this individual who, passing
> from the countryside, saw the dancing there in front of the church of
> Santa Maria. So he took off his saddlebag from his shoulders, because he
> was returning from the fields, and he left his saddlebag and joined in the
> dance. And there's a verse from the dance that they still sing today:

Dance, dance now those dances that are yours;
And when ours will come, we will dance then.[7]

And the allusion was this: don't mix the living with the dead in the
dance. And at a certain point when he was dancing, he rested—he felt
that their shoulders were empty. And then he understood that he had
entered the dance of the dead. And so before they could realize it, he left
the dance, he put his saddlebag on his shoulder and came back to town.
And so he saved himself.[8]

Gesuino Torres, a man who is unusually devoted to the Madonna di
Runaghes, told the following story of hidden treasure:

The people were greatly devoted to the Madonna di Runaghes. In the
old, old, old times, there was a nuraghe there. Anna's great grandfather
found money there. That would be her grandmother's father. He died
when he was old and deaf; but they say he made a deal with the devil for
this money. Who knows how he did it? He did this and this and this; he
found this money buried in that field. And he began to buy land, and
became rich.[9]

Stories of buried treasure near nuraghi or shaft-tombs are common in
Sardinia, but I was not able to collect other variants of this particular tale.
The legend may be peculiar to Uncle Gesuino, a renowned raconteur whose
longstanding rivalry with Anna and her family may have led him to invent
the tale.

The connection between Santa Maria, the dead, rain, and buried treasure
has been researched by Vittorio Lanternari (1984), who has posited a link
between certain contemporary folk legends and prehistoric Sardinian religion. According to his thesis, archeological remains show water, fertility, and
a cult of the dead to have been prominent elements in pre-Christian Sardinian
religion. Because peasants often found coins, pot shards, and other archeological evidence on ancient sites of worship, the idea of buried treasure also
became associated with these locations (Lanternari, 1984:144). If this thesis
is correct, then the connection between Santa Maria and a pre-Christian deity
worshipped at the same location suggested in the historical section of this
chapter becomes more plausible.

While the first two legends portray Santa Maria as a benefactress who
helps the devout and sends water in times of drought, the later legends seem
to imply a different set of associations, at least with the locale of the little
chapel. Places said to be haunted by the dead are often on the borders of the
known, inhabited world. The chapel of Santa Maria is located in just such a
place: a rise that stands on the edge of town, between the inhabited area and
the countryside. If we recall the very strict division of town and countryside
characteristic of Sardinian culture, we may see that Santa Maria falls into a
kind of gray area between the two, a place between the worlds of nature and
culture. It is fitting that the dead should be reported to dance in exactly this
liminal place—that Santa Maria, itself between two worlds, should be inter-

preted in legend as a gateway to the supernatural world as well. It is interesting to note that I collected one report of UFOs in Monteruju, and not
surprisingly, my source reported sighting them flying over Santa Maria.

In addition to the above legends, Santa Maria di Runaghes is commonly
reported to have performed a number of miraculous cures. These reports are
essentially personal narratives of healing, or reports of the healings of neighbors and relatives. Among the narratives I collected were the following: the
Virgin is said to have cured a paralyzed, mute child; saved a young man who
was working as a prison guard from a nervous breakdown after the inmates
tried to put him in the oven; healed another child who was on the point of
death from some illness; and helped women suffering from infertility. A like-
ness of her in a woman's home is supposed to have kept an unsteady wall
from crumbling, and she miraculously healed a man and his wife who had
fallen sick at the same time.[10]

The most widely known report of the Virgin's healing power involves the
miraculous cure of the sheep of Giovanni Antonio Rassu, which were dying
of a pestilence, in 1934. The legend is well known largely because of the
efforts of Uncle Rassu to commemorate the feat through an ex-voto and a
photograph showing a statue of the Virgin in a field surrounded by sheep.
She is flanked by Uncle Rassu and his wife—though it is likely that the photo
of his wife is superimposed on the image, as she had in fact died some years
before the supposed miracle took place. This photograph was reproduced in
postcard form and is in the possession of a number of families in Monteruju,
mostly those who are kin to Uncle Rassu or his wife. That the legend is
closely connected with the photograph in the imagination of many is clear in
the way it is usually narrated; reference is openly made to the arrangement of
subjects in the photograph. While visiting the chapel of Santa Maria with me,
Anna Nieddu recalled the ex-voto and the miracle:

> A: There was the one about my aunt and the sheep, because her sheep
> were always getting sick. They took out the Madonna—out in a field near
> here—and there's the husband and my aunt, with the Madonna and the
> sheep. This was my father's sister and her husband.
>
> S: Did the sheep get better?
>
> A: Well, I don't know; I guess they did. They were dying on her. And this
> [ex-voto] was for grace received.

The odd thing about the photograph is that the statue in the pasture is
not that of Santa Maria di Runaghes. While an older wooden statue of this
Madonna does exist, it is nothing like the small image in the photograph. It is
not clear what statue Uncle Rassu used for the photograph, but it is evident
that he wished the miracle to be connected specifically with Santa Maria di
Runaghes. He even commissioned a painting to be done, in addition to the
photograph, showing the sheep grazing in a pasture near the tiny chapel.[11]

Giovanni Antonio Rassu commissioned a photograph (top) and a painting (bottom) to commemorate the miraculous cure of his sheep by Santa Maria di Runaghes.

Tiu Rassu thus played a key role in forging the connection between Santa Maria and pastoralism. He was well known as a storyteller who could entertain people for hours at work parties with his witty tales, anecdotes, and pieces of memorized poetry. He was also known for taking anecdotes from other sources and telling them as though they had in fact happened to him. It is likely that the legend of Santa Maria healing his sheep was concocted in an analogous manner, patterned after similar stories he had heard.

This interpretation seemed to be an extension of the usual powers attributed to Santa Maria to heal human beings, in which many continue to place great faith. In 1986, for instance, one woman had promised an embroidered altar cloth to her in exchange for improved health; another had made a promise to carry her banner in the procession on the day of the festa, also for health reasons. Perhaps the most touching example in that year was that of a couple whose son was afflicted with leukemia. Each night during the novena, the couple came with the little boy to pray in the chapel, remaining long after all others had left to continue their devotions. Unfortunately, not even these expressions of faith could save the child, who died later that year. But the willingness of the population to turn to this saint over and above any other for intercession in critical circumstances attests to the importance of the Madonna di Runaghes in Monteruju's worldview.

Santa Maria di Runaghes Since 1900

The festa of Santa Maria di Runaghes has undergone a number of permutations during the last century. While change is basic to all festivals, the changes in the Festa of the Madonna di Runaghes have been more numerous and more radical than those in the Feast of the Assumption; they have involved the whole underlying structure of the festival. Moreover, this festa was revived after a period of dormancy between 1971 and 1979. Each successive transformation involved a reshaping of the festival to fit new community needs and values.

At the beginning of the twentieth century,[12] the Festa of Santa Maria di Runaghes was a rather minor affair in the year cycle of Monteruju. It was looked upon chiefly as a religious occasion, an opportunity for pilgrimage to the chapel and for making promessas to the saint. Participants would visit the chapel of Santa Maria every night for the nine nights of the novena, then attend a mass at dawn on September 8. After this mass, a refreshment of wine and cookies was offered to the participants. There were no games, contests, or other celebratory events in connection with the festa.

The organization of the festa of Santa Maria has traditionally been in the hands of women. The principal organizers at the beginning of the twentieth century were two women who belonged to the richest families in town: Annica Arca, the wife of a wealthy landowner; and Anna Filippa Cabras, the sister of a local cleric who eventually became archbishop. In part, the pair paid for some of the expenses of the small festa out of pocket, but a kirka was also involved in gathering ingredients for the cookies. The women would visit each married woman in town and solicit contributions of eggs, flour, or cash; the amount of the contribution varied according to the number of children the woman had. A woman thus paid a kind of toll to the Madonna di Runaghes for each living child she had.

A symbolic connection between the Madonna and human fertility may be postulated from this interchange: the donation could be interpreted as representing a sort of offering in thanks and propitiation for having given birth to a healthy child. In a time when there was no medical help for expectant women and childbirth involved a real risk to the lives of both mother and child, it is understandable that this concern should be made manifest through ritual. The funds for the maintenance of the chapel and the fee for the priest who said the mass and novenas were donated by the Marongios, Monteruju's only titled family.

After the death of Annica Arca in 1929, the community made up a committee of young unmarried women, modeled after the komitatu of the Assumption, to ensure the continuation of the festival. The new komitatu collected grain for the financing of the festa, exactly as the Assumption committee did a few weeks previously, only in lesser quantities, as this festa was shorter and required fewer funds. The shift from a collection of eggs and flour to the collection of wheat was not accidental, however. It corresponded with the period of fascist domination in Italy, during which the government attempted to make Sardinia the breadbasket of Italy, much as the Roman Empire had many centuries before (Boscolo, 1963:49). Since the government was subsidizing the cultivation of wheat, the success of the harvest was of great importance, and as one informant said, "Every scrap of land . . . was given over to the cultivation of grain." Thus, the Festa of the Madonna di Runaghes was reinterpreted in accordance with contemporary concerns and economic conditions. Since wheat was abundant and was being grown as a cash crop, and a successful harvest was crucial to the survival of the community, September 8 became a second festival of thanks and propitiation for the wheat crop.

With the introduction of the komitatu, the ludic elements in this festival began to increase. The ballo tondo was danced in the church square after the procession; a marching band was hired to play during the procession; and one year fireworks were even set off. After the final procession carrying the statue back to the chapel, young men mounted on horseback would ride recklessly through the village to the homes of each obriera, where they would be offered a glass of wine. The horsemen would drink without even dismounting, then rush off to their next destination until all the obrieras had been called upon. While exhibitions of horsemanship are a typical feature of many Sardinian festivals (Costa, 1911:91; Bottiglioni, 1978; Satta, 1982b:98), this type of encounter between eligible bachelors and unmarried young women in the context of festival has not previously been noted. It seems likely that one of the results of the custom was an opportunity for single young people to meet and talk, even if briefly, at a time when contacts between the sexes were limited by cultural restrictions. The appointment of a young girl to the komitatu of Santa Maria may have been a public acknowledgement of her marriageability, much as the appointment of a man to the Assunta's committee is often in recognition of his marriage or some other milestone in his lifecycle.

The focus of these festivities, however, was not the tiny chapel of Santa Maria but instead the central square in front of St. Martin, the parish church. Before 1981, the nightly novenas and the *missa de s'aurora* were held at Santa Maria. Many villagers spent the night at the chapel in vigil, waiting for the early morning mass. Afterwards, the statue of Santa Maria was carried down in procession to the church of St. Martin in the center of the village. It was here that the festivities took place, mostly during daylight hours. In the evening, the procession carried the saint back to her chapel on the edge of town. It was not until the installation of electric lines during the restoration of the chapel that it became feasible to hold the celebration there following the evening mass.

By the early 1970s, the chapel of Santa Maria had deteriorated to the point where the roof was in danger of collapsing. This coincided with a period of general dislike for religious festivals that was sweeping all of Italy (Gallini, 1977:133). In part as a result of the advent of a consumer economy, which disseminated bourgeois models of lifestyle through television and other mass media, and in part through the efforts of the Italian Communist Party, which sought to eliminate traditional religious practices as vestiges of an age of subordination of the peasant classes, year-cycle customs and festivals increasingly came under attack as symbols of backwardness and lack of sophistication. The younger generations especially viewed them with cynicism and disinterest. Anxious to emulate bourgeois city ways, and suffering from a middle generation depleted by emigration, many towns abolished certain festas altogether. The Festa of Santa Maria di Runaghes fell prey to this movement, and for a period of about seven years, from 1971 to 1979, it ceased to be observed.

It is not clear whose idea it was to revitalize the festa. It seems that at some point after 1971, when the festa could no longer be observed because of the dangerous condition of the building, a group of individuals got together and began to collect funds for the restoration of the chapel. Some women in this group had been on the last committee for Santa Maria and continued to contribute a yearly quota that was spent on repairs. In addition, four men formed a self-appointed committee to direct the restoration work. These included Leonardo Piras, a town clerk with many years of administrative experience; Sandro Solinas, a member of the town council; Leonardo Ledda, a policeman; and Gesuino Torres, whose devotion to Santa Maria is well known in the village. The restoration work was financed entirely out of local contributions, and the labor was provided on a voluntary basis by the men of Monteruju. After several years of work on the building, it was ready for inauguration in September of 1981.

In 1979 and 1980, the committee offered a mass at the partially restored chapel; but because the renovation was not yet complete, no celebratory elements were included in the observation of the festa and no new committee was appointed. After 1980, the committee of oberaios for the festa was modified to include both unmarried men and women, although women would always hold the titles of prima and secunda (the assistant of the prima, literally "the second one") and would continue to be more active in the planning and organization of the festa.

While the inauguration of the chapel in 1981 was a small affair, with a refreshment of wine and cookies analogous to those at the turn of this century, each subsequent festa has been more elaborate than the last. The wiring of the building for electricity during the remodeling has permitted the installation of outdoor floodlights, which allow the festivities to continue into the late evening hours. In 1982, circle dancing was successfully introduced as part of the evening's festivities; and since 1984, the committee has been sponsoring a communal feast of boiled mutton, potatoes, and cheese in addition to the wine and cookies offered previously. Finally in 1987, an antique statue of Santa Maria, which had been abandoned in a local cellar, was restored and reconsecrated. The introduction of each of these features of the festa is treated in detail below.

Since its revival, the festa has grown in scope and has met with great enthusiasm from the general population. Some have termed it "the most heartfelt of all festas" in Monteruju. While the Assumption so often arouses negative comments when mentioned, informants had mostly positive comments about Santa Maria: "Nice festa, better than Mesaustu!" one man said to me as I passed in front of his house on the morning after the festival. Although it competes with the large festa of the Madonna di Seunis in nearby Thiesi, virtually everyone in Monteruju attends the festa at Santa Maria. Recent years have seen the increasing attendance of outsiders, most of whom are attracted by the lights and noise as they drive past on the state road. But this is no *festa de forastieri* (festa for outsiders), but a community event that involves the whole town on an intimate level. Now that the occasions for work parties with neighbors no longer exist, the festa of Santa Maria is per-

---

The Festa Today

The present schedule of the festa may be delineated as follows:

Aug. 30–Sept. 7	6:00 PM	Vespers, mass, singing of gosos (hymns)
Sept. 7	8:00 PM	Procession taking S. Maria to town
Sept. 8	6:00 PM	Procession bringing S. Maria back to chapel
	7:00 PM	Mass
	8:00 PM	Refreshment served; feasting begins
	9:30 PM	Evening entertainments: music, circle dance, singing

haps the only occasion for the whole town to come together and celebrate as a community. The communal feasting, followed by the circle dance, in which virtually all able community members participate regardless of skill, create a feeling of communitas which is often missing in this highly dependent village of commuters and isolated nuclear family households. The festa fills an important need in the life of Monteruju that is not met by any other year-cycle custom.

The Ritual

The religious aspect of this festa is obvious even to the casual observer, in contrast to the Assumption, in which secular entertainments often obscure the religious function. During the novena preceding the festa, prayer and devotion are the main objectives of the faithful who make daily pilgrimages to the little chapel to hear mass and vespers. Most of these are women and their elementary-school-aged children. The few men who are present during the novena are usually fathers, husbands, or brothers of the worshippers who have given them a lift to the chapel in their cars. Typically, they do not enter the chapel but lounge around on the tiny piazza in front of the church, smoking or chatting. Men do enter the chapel during the day of the festa itself to hear the religious service, but the novena is obviously perceived as part of women's religious behavior. Since the service is lengthy, the small children who accompany their mothers are not required to stay inside but are permitted to play in and around the chapel. This they do with great force and abandon, and there is a good deal of running in and out of the chapel throughout the function. Greater attention is expected of adolescent girls who attend with their mothers or schoolmates. Boys generally cease attending the novena around the age of six or seven.

The *promessa*, or promise of devotion to the saint in exchange for some grace or favor, is central to the festa of Santa Maria. While not all participants in the novena have made such promises, many have. Pleas for restored or improved health which result in ex-votos are usually made in connection with the novena; daily pilgrimage to Santa Maria and participation in the novena are usually integral parts of the promessa. Even outside the framework of the promessa, personal devotion to the Madonna di Runaghes is very high in Monteruju and is especially obvious during the days preceding the festa. Large numbers of women bring flowers from their gardens to decorate the shrine; others place personal gifts of jewelry on the statue of the Virgin. While most men do not participate in this type of behavior, the town basket weaver and rope maker gave the Virgin a *trizza* (corn dolly) in homage, as he had given to prominent individuals in the community. Throughout the festa, while the statue of the Virgin is on display before the altar, it is common to see the faithful touch the statue and cross themselves as a sign of piety.

Unlike everyday services and masses for other festive occasions, the Mass and panegyric for Santa Maria are read in Sardinian. This is another example of the growing desire for Sardinian regional identity—as opposed to identification with the dominant Italian culture—which is sweeping the island. Although particularly concentrated in urban centers among bourgeois liberals and national separatists (Gallini, 1977), the results of this movement are increasingly being felt even in small rural communities such as Monteruju. In this case, the insistence on the use of Sardinian in the liturgy serves to bind the community together, calling attention to the common language bond, hearkening back with nostalgia to earlier times, and emphasizing the intimate, "down-home" nature of this festival.

The service is followed by the singing of a gosos in Sardinian to Santa Maria di Runaghes. These hymns, though different for each individual patron saint, are widespread in Sardinia and are usually performed during religious functions of patronal festas.[13] The content of these hymns "may be characterized by its laudatory, narrative, descriptive and symbolic aspects, aimed at displaying the merits, virtues and graces" of the saint involved (Atzori and Satta, 1980:41). Gosos were introduced to Sardinia from Spain during the period of Spanish domination. Early examples were in fact in Castilian, though they seemed to have quickly diffused through the island, and hundreds of examples in Sardinian dialects were produced between the sixteenth and seventeenth centuries. They may be "classed among the vast body of sacred folk poetry so widely diffused in European folklore from the Middle Ages onward" (ibid.). They serve an important function in Sardinian folk religion: they provide a simple, easily memorized form for the spreading of religious notions on the lives of saints to a once largely illiterate population.

The gosos of Nostra Segnora di Runaghes, as it is called, is distributed on mimeographed, typed sheets to the faithful during the novena. Most women, however, have little need for the written words, as they have memorized the hymn. A full translation follows.

Although gosos continue to be sung for many rural patronal festas, in the singing of this characteristic hymn for Santa Maria we can discern a determination to retain customs now seen as symbolic of Sardinian ethnicity and culture.

Two processions are involved in the festa of Santa Maria: one on the evening of September 7, carrying the statue by candlelight to the parish church, and another the afternoon of September 8, carrying her back to the chapel before the festivities. Both processions are quite short and direct, and they do not complete the circuitous route through the town of the Assunta's procession. The scheme of the procession is similar to that of the Assumption, with the children at the head of the procession, followed by the women, the clergy, and the statue on her litter. The general population follows close behind. In this smaller procession, however, there is no marching band or peasant costumes and the mood is more somber than the disorderly chatter of the Assumption. One reason for this may be the lack of participation by outsiders; the festa of Santa Maria di Runaghes is so small that few non-natives attend, and it lacks the spectacle that attracts tourists to the Madonna di Seunis in Thiesi, which takes place at the same time.

Gosos of Our Lady of Runaghes

REFRAIN (repeated after each verse):
Created for our benefit,
For light, consolation and joy
Pray for us, Mary,
Known as "de Runaghes."

Conceived in St. Anne's bosom,
Spotless, totally pure and unsullied
By any sin, great or small,
From the great celestial arc,
You are full and fresh.

Beloved of St. Anne,
Descended from David,
More resplendent than the sun,
You appear so luminous,
Banishing the dark
And very long night.

From that first instant
Of your holy being,
[You have been] spotless and without
    original sin,
Shining with grace, preserving
All things immaculate.

In the month preceding
Your birth,
The divine parliament
Filled you with all eminent virtues,
So you could be born more adorned.

When you were born, Lady,
And appeared to the world,
The depths were closed
To the sinful soul;
Blessed for us the hour
And day that you were born.

As soon as you were born,
Giving the enemy
Of slaves of Hell,
You broke our chains,
You rose above any punishment
Marked with victory.

The instant you were born
Adorned with so many gifts,
With melodies and music,
You presented yourself to life,
And from the heavens opened
Doors which [previously] had been
    closed.

God gave you life
To open the heavens for us,
Praised from eternity
And kept with zeal,
And adorned with the immaculate
    veil.

Favored daughter of the Father,
Mother of the Redeemer,
Pure bride of the Spirit
With pure divine love,
Song of every prophet,
Our much-desired light.

Resplendent dawn of light and justice,
You overcame the evil
Of the infernal serpent
And consoled every living being
With sublime mercy.

The triumphs of divine virtue
Acclaim you queen
Of all kingdoms;
You were given to us
That we might be happy.

And on your nativity
We worship you with our hearts
We are all with you
Worshipping the Trinity
To celebrate you
In the longed-for homeland.

Now you are exalted
Above any hierarchy
Pray for us, Mary,
Called "de Runaghes."

The Celebration

While the Festival of the Assumption involves a number of public enter-tainments open to all community members and outsiders, combined with simultaneous private celebrations (feasting, drinking, homecomings) open only to family members and friends, at Santa Maria the community partici-pates in these celebratory aspects publicly, as a whole. The communal feast-ing, dance, and singing are powerful unifying forces because nearly everyone participates together, at the same time, and in each other's presence. In the case of this festa, Monteruju's small size works in its favor; the community is small enough to feel like a large family. The festa is often likened to a family affair: "It's like a wedding, or a party," one woman said.

If, for the purposes of the festa, Monteruju can be likened to a family, then the same principles should apply to its operation as apply to the Sardinian peas-ant family in general. One important principle of the peasant family (not lim-ited by any means to Sardinia) is its economic self-sufficiency: the peasant family functions as an independent economic unit, ideally producing most of the goods for its own consumption. In contrast to the Assumption, in which most of the "goods" (entertainers, performers, sporting events, etc.) must be brought in from outside the community, for the festa of Santa Maria efforts are made to keep all of the elements which make up the celebratory aspect internal to the community. This puts the festa closer to the older model of festival opera-tion, wherein the community joined in a joyous consumption of its own surplus production. The benefits of this system for a small community like Monteruju are twofold: the festival is kept within the economic possibilities of the commu-nity, and the interdependence of community members is highlighted—de-emphasizing, for the short span of the festa, the town's growing dependence on the world outside. The economic and the symbolic are closely intertwined.

Decorations for Santa Maria di Runaghes are much less elaborate than for the Assumption. A string of colored lights is draped outside the little chapel, and a floodlight is rigged to provide lighting during the evening festivities, but this is only done on the day of the feast, September 8. During the days of the novena, the church is kept supplied with fresh flowers, which are replaced regu-larly. While for the Assumption flowers are brought in from the florist shops in nearby towns, the flowers for Santa Maria come from people's gardens. "Santa Maria wants wildflowers, simple flowers," people explained. Wildflowers and garden flowers—daisies, carnations, zinnias—are thought to be more appropri-ate to Santa Maria because of her rural character and obvious connection with nature. Even the banner carried in procession is embroidered with wildflowers. This symbolic connection also has an economic aspect: it eliminates the cost of hothouse-grown flowers from the festival's budget and allows this important component to be provided without resorting to outside establishments.

On the morning of September 8, male oberaios for the festa are busy stringing up lights and setting up long trestle tables around the tiny chapel of Santa Maria. The tables are arranged so as to leave a large central space in front of the church for the circle dancing. They are covered with paper to facilitate cleanup. The oberaios also set up four or five large kettles on outdoor gas burners under the portico of the chapel. These are for cooking of mutton stew for the feast following the service.

The feast has now become the focal point of the celebration. Except for the cookies and wine, which are needed in such huge quantities that they must be bought from suppliers in nearby towns, all of the elements in the menu are donated locally. The sheep to be slaughtered for the stew and the cheese which is served afterwards are given by obrieri on the committee or by families in lieu of a cash offering. Potatoes and onions, which are added to the stew for flavoring, come from local gardens, as do the characteristic herbs used in seasoning: basil, bay laurel, mint, and fennel. The feast features as its primary components the two most important products of the shepherding industry: meat and cheese. In consuming these together in a public ritual, the community performs an important symbolic act of thanks, propitiation, and communion with the saint.

The communal aspect of feasting is very important. While for the Assumption it is customary for families to eat together in their homes in a ritualized version of the everyday noon meal, at Santa Maria it is rare to see people eating in family groups. Instead, tables tend to be composed of groups of friends and age-mates. There are usually one long table of elderly men, several groupings of old women, various clusters of same-sex friends in their middle years, and one large mixed group of teenage boys and girls. The only family groups are mothers with children so young they require help eating. Older children seem not to eat at all, but instead run around playing. Nobody eats alone; in fact, this contradicts the spirit and purpose of the occasion. This was brought home to me quite clearly in 1986 when, in the middle of photographing and recording events, I tried to grab a bite to eat while taking pictures. No sooner had I climbed up on a wall with my cameras, bread, and cheese than Elena, the prima, approached me and physically hauled me down. "What are you doing?" she scolded. "You must not eat alone; this is the festa!" In spite of my protests, she found a place for me at one of the crowded tables where my women friends were sitting, made me sit down among them, and handed me a plate heaped with steaming mutton.

After the feast is over, the music and dancing begin. No large outside rock band is brought in for this occasion; Monteruju has its own small musical ensemble that plays a variety of popular tunes as well as the traditional music required for the circle dance. The cost for their services is minimal (550,000 lire, or about $600, in 1986) compared with the expense of hiring a professional, well-known group through one of the island's booking agencies. Well aware of the diversities in musical tastes in the community, the group plays selections to appeal to everyone. Early in the evening, ballroom dance tunes alternate with Sardinian music; towards the small hours, after the middle-aged and elderly have retired for the night, the band plays modern hit tunes to appeal to the younger crowd. Because the chapel is relatively far from the inhabited area, the rock music does not annoy those who are sleeping, as occurs during the festa of the Assumption. Through this strategy, all the age groups in the community are satisfied.

The ensemble's music is intended mainly as an accompaniment to dance rather than as a spectacle in and of itself, as in the case of a concert. People in fact dance throughout the night while the group is playing. Most forms of ballo civile, or ballroom dance, draw their devotees from particular age groups: waltzes and polkas attract couples aged forty and older, while rock tunes appeal to teenagers and young couples. But all age groups join together in dancing the ballo tondo, or circle dance. In the traditional form of this dance, men and women alternately join hands and form a circle. They make a shuffling movement with their feet in time to the music, while the upper half of the body is supposed to remain nearly motionless. Some skill and practice are necessary to execute the ballo tondo properly, and at one time the most skilled dancers in the community exhibited their prowess during festas. But the ballo tondo as it is performed now at Santa Maria does not demand such talent. In fact, nearly everyone can participate, from skilled dancers of the older generation to children who cannot master the basic steps. Since the circle quickly becomes a fast-moving line spiraling in on itself, the unskilled are simply pulled along. The ballo tondo is performed a number of times during the evening, and it does not cease when the older generation has retired, but alternates with rock selections. This suggests that, at least on this occasion, it is a powerful symbol of community also for the generation under thirty.

In contrast to the celebratory aspects of the Assumption, those of Santa Maria are much more participatory in nature. At Santa Maria, the clear-cut distinction between audience and performers that characterizes the spectacular entertainments of the Assumption is absent. Rather than being passively entertained by staged events, the townspeople actively participate; they create their own entertainment. Throughout the evening one is likely to find small groups singing rowdy drinking songs, playing *morra* (a gambling game),[14] and otherwise amusing themselves. The community has thus recreated for itself a festa with many of the features of festas before the imposition of the new cultural model, which removed folklore from the province of daily life and put it on a stage. The participatory nature of these entertainments carries a strong symbolic charge. For the old timers, they are reminiscent of the old model of the festa which they recall from their youth; for younger people, they represent something different from the usual festa, with its rock concerts and carnival aspects. In both cases, they create a sense of unity that transcends generational boundaries.

∽҃Ж∾

Gender Roles and Power on the Komitatu

Since the revival of the festa the komitatu has consisted of both men and women, but women continue to hold the reins of power in the organization of the festa. In spite of the equal numbers of men and women on the committee, women outnumbered the men at meetings. While the men tended to sit around the edges of the room or lean against the wall, the women sat around the meeting table and participated fully in the discussions. The group performing the kirka consisted of six women and two men, who dropped out soon after starting. During the kirka, a good deal of joking took place based on the fact that a group of women was begging for money. "What will you give us in return, eh?" a few male homeowners asked good-naturedly. This kind of sexual banter, which does not normally take place between male and female acquaintances in this usually restrained culture, can occur within the context of the festival kirka because the usual roles are reversed: women are in a position of power, and the householder is bound by the rules of his culture to accede to their demands. The statement is interpreted as a joke rather than as a sexual advance.

The division of labor on the committee, however, reflects traditional gender roles in Monteruvian households. The festa is thought of as a large party; thus, women plan, organize, and prepare many aspects related to food and drink. They also take care of cleaning the church, buying necessary groceries and supplies (e.g., paper plates, napkins, etc.), arranging flowers, and cleaning up after the merrymaking. Male obrieri set up the heavy tables, electrify the square, and butcher and cook the sheep. While cooking is usually a feminine occupation, outdoor cooking over an open fire is associated with the life of a shepherd and so is perceived as a male task.

In many ways, the festa can be seen as a coming together of polar opposites in Sardinian society: nature and culture, the fields and the village, male and female. Women move from the cultural space of the home and village to the natural space of the country chapel, where through work they impose a cultural order—cleaning, decorating, hosting, and bringing the civilizing reciprocal relations of the town into the natural world.

The prima's role includes most of the planning and administrative duties connected with the festa. Since the festa's revival, the position of prima has been particularly powerful. The brief hiatus in its celebration permitted the total reformation of the festa and, until a new basic program structure had been established, gave considerable freedom to the prima and the komitatu to structure the festa according to their needs and tastes. In fact, the present form of the festa is due largely to the efforts of the first primas, who put their individual stamp on the festival's format. The primas' skill in organizing and managing the festival draws community attention to their abilities and their suitability for public office. While women do not serve on the komitatu with the express purpose of obtaining political power, their role within the festival allows them a considerable say in administration and decision making. Those showing exceptional skill in these areas, or those who give the community a wildly successful festival, may then rise to power in the non-ritual world.

Natalie Zeamon Davis (1978) has noted that during the transition from the agrarian to the urban industrial order in sixteenth-century France, the trope of "women on top" became associated with carnivalesque festivities,

Outdoor cooking for festivals is perceived as a male task.

misrule, and the triumph of disorder over practicality. Its new role became the promotion of resistance to the established order. While Santa Maria is far from a carnivalesque festival in which we can expect the same kinds of reversals, the dominant role of women in its planning and conception can be viewed as a challenge, within the festive frame, of traditional male dominance in Sardinian society. Without overstepping the bounds of their culture and risking social censure, women participating in the festival's organization can experience control. As in the instance of early modern France cited by Davis, the rise in the importance of women's role in the festival corresponds to a period of transition between the agrarian and the industrial order.

※〆

The Individual, Community, and Tradition

The festa has evolved into its present model because it clearly satisfies certain community needs. But it has done so through the work of a number of individuals whose interpretations of tradition happened to fit with what the town deemed important and aesthetically pleasing.

The creative impact of the individual narrator on tale materials has been well documented in folklore studies (Dégh, 1969; Falassi, 1980). We have seen how Giovanni Rassu was virtually single-handedly responsible for the creation and dissemination of the legend of the miraculous sheep cure. As a tale teller, his contribution to the body of narrative material associated with Santa Maria di Runaghes shaped and influenced the community's perception of her. This is quite in keeping with the documented pattern of storytellers in their communities (Dégh, 1969:176–77).

But just as narrators are personally responsible for introducing creative changes into their materials, individuals are the ones who intentionally modify and reinterpret the parameters of festival each time it is put on. Festivals change—not by themselves or through some mystic communal process, but because interested individuals consciously make innovations. Naturally, the innovations each prima or primu makes are in part determined by his or her own past experiences, ideology, and personality. As with tale tellers, one finds the conservative bearers of tradition, who wish simply to repeat the festival adhering closely to the models of previous years, as well as the innovators, who seek to improve or change an existing tradition by adding, removing, or rearranging elements in the basic program structure. Similarly the changes instituted by each interpreter may be trivial—placing garbage cans at strategic points to facilitate clean-up, for instance—or of great importance, like the institution of the circle dance or the mutton feast (cf. Dégh, 1969:176).

Festivals, of course, change a little each time they occur, and the uncertainty of the outcome of any given festival is part of the genre itself. Not all changes meet with approval from the community. Moreover, in Monteruju, the primu or prima must contend with the will of the rest of the komitatu (itself made up of individuals, of course), which will override suggestions for changes that it considers inappropriate. The community itself will form a reaction to each festival after it occurs that determines which innovations and modifications are likely to be repeated in years to come, and which are likely to be scrapped. Each individual festival, then, must be seen as a combination of traditional elements, which have met the tests of community approbation, and innovative elements based on the obriere maggiore's input and the komitatu's will. It stands to reason that the community will react positively to changes which satisfy certain actual or perceived needs. These, then, are the changes which are most likely to be repeated and to become themselves a part of the festival's basic structure.

The process of innovation and negotiation of change between individual innovators and the community can easily be seen in a festa like Santa Maria di Runaghes, which has only recently been revived. Each year's modifications and the personalities responsible for them are still fresh in people's minds. Also, because of its recent revival, the festa has not yet fossilized into a rigid, prescribed form, as the Assumption has. The prima has more leeway to institute changes as she sees fit.

The personality of the prima, her interest in the festa, and her devotion to the Madonna di Runaghes are of pivotal importance in determining how she will interpret the festa. In order to better understand this process, I will examine in detail a series of innovations in the festa, the primas who instituted them, and the reaction of the community.

The year of the inauguration, the previous committee (which carried over from the last year the festa had been done) chose as prima one of the women of Monteruju with the highest achieved status: Luisa Cossu, a high school teacher with a degree in folklore from the University of Cagliari. Neither particularly religious nor especially interested in the Madonna di Runaghes, Luisa nevertheless felt, as a folklorist, that it was her duty to return the festa to "the way it was traditionally." Because a large number of rural festas in Sardinia are held at the chapels outside the town, she decided it would somehow be "more traditional" to hold the festa up at the chapel rather than in the town square: "From the time we revived the festa, we tried to observe tradition—that is, it seemed more right to us to worship her there *in loco*, and so we said the mass up there" (1986). But for various reasons, some were opposed to this change; so she enlisted the help of the local priest in persuading a recalcitrant population to hold the festa in the country chapel. The first year's festa was "altogether sober," according to Luisa. She had researched the way the festa had been done at the turn of the century, with simply a small refreshment of cookies and wine, and decided to try to reproduce the festa as it had been "originally":

> I remember we bought some sweets and drinks, that is, the classic wavy savoyard; and this is what we offered people. It was altogether sober. . . . We took the Formica kitchen table, the one that's downstairs now, up to Santa Maria, we put the tablecloth on it; everybody was standing up, there wasn't anything there to speak of.

In attempting to return the festa to its "origins," Luisa in fact created a new form, one never before taken by this particular festa. The most important innovation of hers was the shift in the focus of activity from the church square of St. Martin to the chapel at Santa Maria. However, there was some initial resistance to this change. "People were unhappy because they said the old women could not see the Madonna" if she was not carried into town and displayed at St. Martin (Pietrina Secchi, 1986). For many elderly women, it would have been difficult to walk the quarter of a mile uphill to Santa Maria to touch the statue and cross themselves—a common act of worship with any saint's statue on the day of the patronal festa. The following year, the procession was reinstituted: the statue of the Virgin was brought down in the evening on the eve of the festa (September 7) and kept in the church of St. Martin until the next day, when she was carried up to the chapel again just before vespers. Luisa's major innovation was accepted, then, with some modifications in favor of the traditional pattern, which had involved a procession of the Virgin from outside the town to the heart of the community.

The following year, 1982, was a pivotal year for this festival. The prima that year was Anna Nieddu, a woman of 57 who had just moved back to Monteruju after spending most of her life as a domestic servant in Rome. Anna is particularly fond of Santa Maria di Runaghes and has been so since her youth. "I used to always take my vacations in September," she explained, "so I could return for her festa." She is proud of having initiated the custom of giving gifts of jewelry to the statue of the Madonna di Runaghes:

> I gave two rings to the Madonna di Runaghes. I was the first one to do it. The priest protested. He said, "Why put rings on her? When we carry her they fall off," and so on. But now that one is covered, too. And I was the first. First I gave her one. The others are envious, maybe. Now she has rings, she has chains, pins. And before she didn't have a single one.

Anna is devoted to other Madonnas also; she frequently visited the shrine of the Madonna delle Tre Fontane near Rome and has been to Lourdes on pilgrimage as well. But Santa Maria di Runaghes is her special favorite. A perfectionist who had years of experience in domestic service with the organization of large parties for her employers, Anna took her role as prima very seriously and threw herself into it with dedication. Her strong and evident desire for recognition gave her the drive necessary to introduce a number of innovations: the reinstitution of the kirka to finance the festa, a nighttime candlelight procession carrying the Madonna into the town, and the dancing of the circle dance in front of Santa Maria after the refreshment.

The reinstitution of the kirka was the first of Anna's innovations as prima. She realized that to bring her larger plans for the festa into being, more money had to be available than could be generated with only the 20,000 lire quota each obriera contributed:

> This custom [the kirka at Santa Maria] used to exist. Then since they revived [the festival], they didn't do it anymore. The obriere put the quota and that was it. It was no wonder they couldn't put on much of a festa. So when they put me on, I said, "Since you've gone and made me prima, listen: this is how I knew it." We went asking—because nobody denied the Madonna. But I didn't go around begging. I just asked people I was familiar with. And I said to the girls, too—I said, "Ask around the neighborhood." But they were ashamed, because they weren't used to it. They didn't know this from before. So I went looking. And people gave me money: some 10, some 5 [thousand lire]. I certainly didn't expect much, because I knew everyone lived off pensions; but nobody denied me. When the festa was over, there at Santa Maria, the men would come up and give me money. I was able to gather a good bit. In fact there were 25,000 lire left over.

With the funds she obtained, Anna set about shaping the festa to her specifications. One form of recreation which had always been particularly dear to her heart was the circle dance. "In the old days, they used to dance the ballo sardo on the square every night [of the Assunta's festival]. That really was a good time, not like these kids today," she explained. Like her father and mother, Anna is an exceptionally good dancer of the ballo sardo. She missed the dwindling opportunities to practice her skill once she returned to her home village. The idea came up as she discussed plans for the festa with another obriere to organize a circle dance at Santa Maria. "It was almost as a lark," she explained. She persuaded this man to use his skills as an electrician to rig up a floodlight outside the chapel. Then she set to work convincing two local musicians, sons of a neighbor, to play some traditional dance music after the refreshment. The result was a smashing success. "They were doing the ballo sardo 'til two in the morning," she told me. "People were coming up to me after the mass and handing me money."

Evidently the reintroduction of this tradition struck a positive chord with many community members. Other middle-aged people who remembered the circle dances from their youth also missed this essential (to them) element of festivity as its importance in the festival of the Assunta decreased. They, too, welcomed this new opportunity to display their skill and recapture the experiences of their youth. The ballo tondo is not limited to older adults, though; nearly everyone who is able to joins in the dance, regardless of their skill. Young people literally dance hand-in-hand with old people in a very concrete expression of communitas. It is one of the few occasions when the strict age and sex boundaries dividing the village are temporarily suspended, and informal interaction between these groups takes place (Atzori and Satta, 1980:176–77). The ballo tondo became a symbolic enactment of Monteruju's fragile identity as a community; for this reason, it has become an integral part of the new festa at Santa Maria.

Another innovation in the festival program made during 1982 was the institution of a candlelight procession bearing the statue of the Madonna to the main church in the village on the night of September 7, the eve of the festa. This was not entirely due to the efforts of Anna Nieddu but was actually suggested to her by Don Chessa, a missionary priest from Monteruju who had just returned from many years of service to a congregation in Chile. The introduction of elements by Church hierarchy is nothing new in the history of festival; Catholic patronal festivals owe their present form largely to such instances (Atzori and Satta, 1980:175). But these innovations remain unsuccessful unless they satisfy some sort of community need. Anna's enthusiasm for the idea insured its success and implementation, however, and the aesthetically pleasing quality of the twilight procession, with its bobbing candles, was a success with the community. The local clergy retain a great influence on festive forms, of course, and there is often a power struggle between the komitatu, for whom the festa is a ritual sphere of action involving the community as a whole, and the clergy, who see it as an occasion for the reaffirmation of the relationship between the individual and God (ibid., 174). But despite the historic efforts of the Church to impose its models on the community, community will usually prevail with time. Anna, for example, suggested to the priest that the mass be held outdoors in front of the chapel on the day of the festa:

> I wanted to have the mass on the outside plaza [of S. Maria]. "Why don't
> we do it on the square?" I said to [the priest]. "Oh, no," he said, "Because
> if a donkey passes by, everyone turns around; a goat goes by, everyone
> turns around. . . ." He didn't listen to me about that. But last year [1985]
> they started doing it outside, and I noticed nobody turns around.

Largely due to Anna's efforts, the festa acquired most of its present components in 1982. The success of her innovations can be attributed in part to her
own skill as an interpreter of cultural symbols, such that her ideas were well
in keeping with general community tastes and expectations, and partly to the
style with which she introduced them. Although eager for recognition, she
eschewed an authoritarian style of imposing her will on the komitatu and the
community—a style totally alien to the cultural environment. "The one who
is in charge of [everything] is the prima," Anna explained to me, "but you ask
for advice." She relied on her contacts with friends and neighbors to obtain
help in bringing about wanted changes: "I just asked people with whom I was
in confidence." In this way, it was not only her individual will that was done,
but also that of the community.

In 1984, a third important innovation was introduced: a community
feast of boiled mutton and vegetables in addition to the refreshment of wine
and cookies. This was not the result of the innovation of an individual prima
but came instead from the komitatu itself. The prima in 1984 was a teacher
and part-time university student whose schedule did not permit her much
time to dedicate to the planning of the festa. That year, several shepherds on
the committee offered to contribute sheep for a feast in lieu of the regular
quota. Rather than being sold and the proceeds used for festival expenses, the
sheep were butchered and cooked in large kettles over portable gas burners in
the portico of the chapel. The male obrieri supervised the cooking. The
resulting stew was the basis of a feast that was served to the whole community after the mass.

The idea of the community feast grew from what is in essence a local
custom among shepherds: to celebrate some private event, a shepherd will
sometimes slaughter a sheep, cook it, and invite male friends to feast on it. In
1984, one shepherd on the committee volunteered to give such a party for the
other male obrieri once the work of preparing for the festa was done. But
Leonardo Ledda, a 50-year-old policeman serving on the committee that
year in place of his son, who was working on the continent, objected:

> I said, "Listen, Antonio, you won't accomplish anything by killing one
> sheep. Instead of doing one [sheep], let's make the festa and we'll all give
> sheep." I had said this myself. So that's how it went.

The committee liked and accepted Leonardo's idea, and seven obrieri agreed
to donate sheep for the celebration.

The communal feast of boiled mutton was a tremendous success with the
community. Not only did the town unite in the festive act of consuming food;
the symbolic addition of the mutton feast also tied the festa in fully with the

seasonal and economic cycle of Monteruju. The shepherds' feast of mutton stew and cheese publicly celebrated the importance of pastoralism as the town's economic base. The beginning of the pastoral year cycle could now be marked by the ritual slaughter and consumption of the sheep too old to endure another winter, and all this could be done in honor of Santa Maria, bringer of rain and green pastures, guardian of health and fertility, and protectress of Monteruju. With the addition of the feast, Santa Maria became a symbolically satisfying package that met a number of community needs: the need to affirm and celebrate the prevalent economic activity in a meaningful way; the need for community interaction beyond the level of immediate family; and the need to preserve and display a sense of community identity and independence in the face of growing dependence on the outside world.

A final step in the revitalization of this festival occurred in 1987, under the direction of prima Marta Pinna: the restoration and reconsecration of the original statue of Santa Maria di Runaghes. This wooden statue, depicting an adolescent Madonna, probably dates from the early eighteenth century but had been out of use since 1909, the date a new plaster statue was acquired.

The original statue of
Santa Maria di Runaghes

Since the 1950s the wooden statue was no longer kept in the chapel but resided in a private home belonging to a devotee. There the statue had gradually deteriorated.

Marta got the idea for the restoration from visiting friends, who saw the country chapel and noticed that the new plaster statue belonged to a different period from the sanctuary. Marta explains:

> I said, "We have the [original] statue; if you want to see it, I'll take you there." A few days later, the woman in whose house the statue was came to [my workplace], and the other obriere came. I remembered about my friends, and I said, "Listen, Maria, why don't you give the statue back to the church?" And she goes, "Well, I'd sure like to bring her back to the church, but she ought to be restored." So I go, "Look, you say the word, and I'll take care of it, me and the other obriere." And that's how the thing got started.

The statue was professionally cleaned and restored, and new clothing was made for it in the style of the original (but faded and torn) garments. It was reconsecrated by the parish priest and carried in procession to its new home in the chapel. The restoration and reconsecration of the antique statue provided the crowning touch to the festival's revival. A testament to the importance of Santa Maria di Runaghes for Monteruvians, the statue also symbolically represents the Virgin's nativity and the beginning of a new year cycle: "Don't you see she's undeveloped, a little girl?" women devotees point out, sometimes referring to the statue as "Maria Bambina." Since the obriere for this festival are unmarried, and, at least in theory, virgins at the beginning of their life cycle, they can indeed be said to embody Santa Maria and the promise of fertility and plenty that she brings.

Santa Maria di Runaghes is presently enjoying a period of revival in Monteruju. Once a small festival, it has grown steadily in importance throughout this century, blossoming after its revival in the early 1980s. Part of its success is due to its relationship to the growing importance of pastoralism in Monteruju. Its success can also be attributed to its relatively low budget and the committees' attempts to keep as many expenditures as possible within the community itself. Unlike the Assumption, celebratory features have not been removed from the participatory sphere; rather, the festival serves as a forum for the recreation of many participatory activities once associated with other festivals. On the whole, this festival is more satisfying to the community than the Assumption. Because of this, it has become an important symbol of community in this divided and conflicted town.

Notes

[1] According to Angius (1833:264), Santa Maria was one-half mile from the inhabited area of Monteruju, but since 1833 the town has expanded in the direction of the chapel.

[2] This was probably sometime after 1866, when, after the unification of Italy, laws were passed concerning the location of graveyards outside town limits for sanitary reasons. At this time, there were no laws protecting nuraghi, as archeological remains, from the depredations of

those who wanted to use the cut stones for other constructions. Presently, all nuraghi are protected by law as historic monuments.

3 Piras (1961:194) claims that during the period of Aragonese domination, "Santa Maria," which had been the common title of the Virgin during the whole medieval period, was changed to the Spanish form, "Nuestra Señora." Churches and cults dating from this period use the title "Nostra Segnora." This assertion proves little about the festa, however, since both titles are currently in use.

4 The novena, a period of nine days of prayer preceding a feast, originated in pre-Christian times from the Greek and Roman custom of nine days' mourning following a death. It attained wide popularity during the medieval period, especially in connection with Marian feasts and saints' days. It came to be a time of special supplication in which the devout sought favors . . . through the intercession of saints. Usually the favors have to do with the restoration of good health. For a description of the novenas connected with Marian worship in modern times, see Beinert (1978) and DeRosa (1981).

5 See, for instance, Dundes and Falassi (1975) for a description of this type of custom in Tuscany.

6 Similar to Aarne-Thompson Type 770, "Soeur Beatrice," in which a nun leaves her convent with her lover and the Virgin takes her place while she is away. Later the nun returns and repents her actions (Aarne, 1981, Motif K1841, "Virgin Mary substitutes for a mortal"). No examples listed for Sardinia or any region of Italy in the *Inventario Nazionale*.

7 The verse in Sardinian is, as recited by my informant, is: "*Ballade, ballade como, a sos ballos ki sun bostros; Kand'ada bennere sos nostros, amus a ballare nois.*"

8 The legend of the dance of the dead (Motif E493) is widespread in European tradition. Usually those who join in pay with their lives, or return hundreds of years later to find their friends and relatives dead and the world changed. Twelve other examples have been recorded in Sardinia, but the *Inventario Nazionale per tipi, motivi o argomenti* does not list examples from other regions of Italy. However, eleven examples of legends of the dead appearing around chapels or churches have been recorded from other Italian regions.

9 Motifs G303.22, "Devil as helper," and M210, "Bargain with the devil." Legends of buried treasure (*siddadu* in Sardo) are common not only in Sardinia (See Enna, 1984), but in Italian tradition generally: the *Inventario Nazionale* lists 21 examples from various regions of Italy. E. Delitala has noted that treasures are often said to be located in nuraghi, dolmens or caves, and are guarded by giants, fairies or devils in many Sardinian legends (Delitala, 1963).

10 Not all who hear these legends believe them. For example, Gavina Musio's daughters, who were present during the telling of some of these tales, scoffed at them: "What did that resolve?" one said. "The illness left the child feebleminded, and that prison guard was as weird before they put him in the oven as after."

11 As Dégh and Vázsonyi (1977) have noted, the legend is in many instances accompanied by the "negative legend," a refutation of the occurrence recounted in the legend. As in the above instances, there are those who dispute the miracle altogether. Nando Manzella, who had worked for Uncle Rassu as a tenant-shepherd for many years, claimed no miracle had ever occurred:

> I was [working for Uncle Rassu] four years. And in [19]34, between '34 and '35, [his sheep] were dying. And many died. But I didn't see any miracle. I'm telling you the truth; I didn't. Because afterwards I was there again another time, and they were dying just the same, in the same way. I was older then; I'm talking about after the war, this last war of [19]45, '46. In '45 they were dying worse than before. . . . And when they stopped dying, thank God, he said it was a miracle; but I didn't believe him, all that bull he was telling me. Tiu Rassu said a lot of these things, because he was an imaginative man.

12 Oral historical accounts do not extend further back than the beginning of the twentieth century, and I was not able to find written accounts describing this festival in Monteruju before then. Naturally, it is likely that it has undergone a number of permutations during the many centuries it seems to have been celebrated, and the form it took early in the twentieth century was only one of many, and not by any means the "original" form.

[13] For the most complete work on the gosos and the related Catalan form *goigs*, see Amades (1940). Also of note are Batle (1924), Moretti (1958), and Ferraro (1891). For an account of the folklorization of religious materials as exemplified by the gosos, see Atzori and Satta (1980), pp. 40–45.

[14] On morra games, see Mathias (1974).

🎀 Chapter 6

The Politics of Festival

Traditionally, anthropologists examining ritual and festival have emphasized their roles as unifying forces within the community. Émile Durkheim believed rituals (including festivals) to be the only means available for communicating the group solidarity he postulated as so important to people (Durkheim, 1915:237–38). Victor Turner, working in Ndembu society (which he characterized as deeply divided by conflict), thought ritual extremely important in providing the Ndembu with evidence of the values they held in common (Turner, 1969). Most Sardinian scholars examining traditional festivals have used this argument as well. Satta (1982b:7) calls them "moments of emerging community solidarity." Gallini (1971:218) sees the festa, particularly the festa longa, as uniting community members in a kind of illusory golden age in which village feuds and disagreements are suspended. Pinna also sees festas as a cohesive force, albeit he comes closer to the truth when he states that the festival "seem[s] to uncover and visibly expose the entire affective web linking all community members . . ." (1971:15). This web, as we have seen in previous chapters, is made up of kin—parafamilial and friendship networks—but characterized by conflicts between age groups, genders, families, and political parties. If during festivals these networks are most clearly articulated, then festivals may serve as moments for emergent conflict as well as solidarity. This may be particularly apparent in times of social transformation, when traditional systems of social exchange have been affected and society is divided by generational and ideological conflicts (cf. Geertz, 1973b:142–169).

Why have many scholars downplayed the role of conflict in festival? One reason may be that the temporary suspension of strife is an important aesthetic component in many festivals. Conflicts do not disappear, but they often must be temporarily suspended for the duration of the celebration. This represents a ludic reversal of the usual, quotidian pattern. During the festa at

113

Santa Maria, for instance, I noticed that one of my friends was repeatedly asked to dance by an ex-boyfriend with whom she had had a stormy breakup. She refused, but the young man insisted; finally she consented. "Why did you dance with him?" I asked her later that evening. "I thought you were still mad at him." "I couldn't refuse," she explained. "This is the festa, it would have been worse if I had refused." It was clear that within the festive frame, the quarrel had to be set aside. The festa did not end the animosity between the two, since it has continued unabated to this day; it did not create agreement where previously there had been discord. It did create an environment in which the appearance of agreement had to be maintained.

When conflicts deeply divide a community, however, they often cannot be completely set aside for the festival. In this chapter, I describe how conflicts emerge in the organizing committees as different factions struggle to control the festival, and how in times of acute political conflict festivals themselves can become political expressions.

༺❀༻

Power and Negotiation in the Komitatu

In Monteruju, conflict is central to both the Assumption and Santa Maria di Runaghes. While conflict is not always apparent during the festival itself, the planning phase of each festival is an arena for playing out conflicts between various community groups. Conflict comes to light as groups struggle to gain control of the festival. This struggle is at the very heart of the folkloric process: it is here that tensions between the individual and the community aesthetic, between tradition and innovation, are resolved.

On the surface, the komitatu seems to be a balanced representation of the community: roughly equal numbers of young and old, men and women. Theoretically, at least, the festa is for everyone. But during the actual meetings, a different balance of power emerges—one that, far from reversing the social order in favor of equality, often reinforces established power relationships. The komitatu can also be a locus for challenging political and social power, with varied results.

The Assumption and Santa Maria festas differ in the types of conflict that they display and the ways in which the conflicts are resolved, but conflict is present in both. In the Assumption, conflict tends to be generational and gender based, as groups engage in a battle of wills to determine the program of the festival. The more powerful elements—the mature, experienced men on the komitatu—are usually successful in imposing their will on the weaker elements. This often creates tremendous resentment among the subordinate groups. The komitatu for the Assunta consists of married and unmarried individuals but is always headed by a married male. In decision making, men consistently outnumbered and overruled women, and the older oberaios dominated the younger ones. The most influential on the komitatu are those who have personal or political contacts who can provide something for the festival free or at a reduced cost. Because, in spite of the many social changes, the ones who tend to have the greatest number of contacts are still males, the balance of power tends to remain squarely in male hands. One man, for instance, knew a florist in Thiesi who could donate flowers for decorating the church in exchange for advertising. This proposal was immediately accepted by the committee. Another man knew the manager of a rock band that was eventually hired to play at the festa in 1986. Since older men tend to have more contacts than younger ones simply because of life experience, the power in the komitatu remains effectively in the hands of the older oberaios.

Men also overrule women with great frequency on the Assumption committee. During one preliminary meeting in 1986, the discussion centered around the choice of musical entertainment for one of the nights of the festival. Almost timidly, Rita Solinas, a 24-year-old office manager who prides herself on being an exponent of women's rights, suggested hiring Elena Ledda, a well-known performer who sings traditional material and accompanies herself on the guitar. The five other young women present supported Rita's proposal. But they were immediately shouted down by the men, who outnumbered them; they did not want a female vocalist, but the traditional quartet of male singers. The women withdrew their suggestion, and no further mention of it was made in the planning of the festival.

On another occasion, a loud discussion pitted men against women on the issue of the preparation of food for the rock band, oral poets, and athletes. Traditionally, performers were not paid in cash but fed by the families of the komitatu. The task of preparing food naturally fell to the wives of the oberaios. Now, although such performers are paid, it is still customary to offer them a meal, and it is the wives of the male oberaios and the female committee members who make the preparations. Rita, again the advocate of women's rights, protested that the band was being paid in cash—why should they be fed, too? Immediately the other women joined her side. But the men quickly asserted that the performers must be offered something, even just sandwiches. "But we're the ones who are going to have to fix them!" Rita shouted. In the end, in spite of Rita's loud protests, tradition triumphed and the women agreed to prepare food for the entertainers.

This power struggle between women and men is not an isolated instance, but part of a phenomenon which repeats itself each year. At the bottom of it lies a kind of resentment many men feel towards the new cultural attitudes women are increasingly demonstrating in respect to festival—attitudes that not only permit women as much enjoyment in the festival as men but also entitle them to this without sacrifice. Leonardo Piras expressed resentment typical of many men in his generation:

> But our wives and daughters, they can't stand to pass these festas cooped
> up in the kitchen. If we were to ask them, they'd say to us: "Hey, buddy,
> it's a holiday for you, and it's one for me, too!"

Generational conflicts also find expression during the organizational phase of the festival because the power of the komitatu rests in the hands of the older members. I recorded the following conversation with Giovanni Secchi, 26 years old and unemployed, and Antonio Piras, a 23-year-old student, only a week before the festival was to occur:

> Antonio: [T]he festa is planned and decided by a privileged few.
>
> Giovanni: We get the rejects. First they decide for the old folks—kantadores, poetas, Duo Puggioni—and with the money that's left over, they say, "Let's find a band for the youngsters." And so it usually happens that the evening with the kantadores is a nice evening because they have the money; and the band is always half-a-shit. . . . These towns are pretty traditionalist and conservative. Before youngsters can get ahead here, we'll need a lot of time.

The problem is a complex one, involving not only generational conflict but also a conflict of values and expectations. At one time, according to Marco Mannu,

> . . . during the time of festas, people had more fun; because it was the only time when, having finished working—working hard, because you worked to eat—that is, those days you had fun, you let go. That's how it was everywhere. . . . Now we have discos, radios, televisions. . . .

And the new lifestyle has created new exigencies. If the rock band is not one of the best, it's lousy; if an entertainment is not new and never before seen, it's boring. "The beauty of that," Nina said once, referring to the introduction of the communal feast for the festa of Santa Maria di Runaghes, "was that it was spontaneous. I think it's a mistake to try to repeat it. They shouldn't try to do the same thing each year; they should do something new every time." Here the clash of values is clear. The old values of cyclic repetition and ritual are being supplanted by the new consumer-economy emphasis on change, innovation, and spontaneity. Yet to organize a festival without some stable elements would be nearly impossible, besides being anathema to another large segment of the population that continues to value traditional entertainments. These tensions, which are products of cultural change, are played out in the conflicts that characterize the komitatu.

There is some evidence that the traditional balance of power on the komitatu of the Assumption is changing, and that the resulting festivals are more satisfying to many. In 1989, for instance, after the designated primu refused to organize the festival, his role was taken over by Francesca Manca, a young woman with substantial organizational and administrative experience, including service on the town council. Francesca put together a festival program which included some traditional features, but also many participatory activities (such as a nature hike and photo exhibit) that appealed across gender and generational boundaries. The festival lasted four days and was judged very successful by many townspeople. As yet, however, there have been no instances of young women appointed prima for the Assumption. Women's power in the festive frame belongs to Santa Maria di Runaghes.

꿍ᴉᴡ

Politics and Conflict in the Komitatu: Santa Maria in 1986

In Monteruju the festa of Santa Maria has been the object of fierce strug-gles for domination by competing groups of women. These conflicts have been of a political and ideological nature, reflecting the two predominant political parties in Monteruju: the Christian Democrats (D.C.) and the Par-tito Socialista Italiano (P.S.I.). The two parties hold contrasting views of festi-vals and public displays in general. While the D.C. has generally valorized these cultural productions for their religious and traditional content, the P.S.I. has tended to see them within a Gramscian framework, wherein festivals belong to an agro-pastoral world which must be left behind in order to achieve true equity and progress. The contrast has been inflamed by church rhetoric characterizing P.S.I. members as "miscreants" who might just do away with festas in the name of progress. While the elimination of festivals has never been a part of the socialist agenda, the P.S.I. administration, while in power, had avoided the use of public funds for festivities and displays, which it considered a waste of taxpayers' money. The priest's rhetoric was intended to frighten many Monteruvians into voting for the D.C., a party tra-ditionally allied with the church in Italy. While many townspeople are in favor of progress, most nevertheless would not like to see the festas neglected or abolished, as for most Monteruvians these events hold powerful emotional and affective associations. The conflict between the two parties began to come to a head in the fall of 1986.

That year, the meetings of the komitatu were dominated by heated politi-cal rivalry between the prima, Elena Tanca, and her secunda, Caterina Man-zella. Elena believed she had been appointed prima because of her political position as vice-mayor: the township had received a government grant for public works, part of which was to be spent on the construction of a square in front of the chapel of Santa Maria; it was thought that Elena could use her political influence to speed the construction of the square. The secunda, Caterina Manzella, belonged to a family of longstanding Christian Demo-crats who had opposed the Socialists' rise to power in 1973 and attempted to thwart their re-election in subsequent years. Caterina's nephew had in fact run against Elena for a seat on the town council in the elections of 1983. The political rivalry between the two women, fueled also by their different person-alities and styles, often erupted in the meetings of the komitatu.

Elena, a 39-year-old teacher, was neither particularly interested in festas nor exceptionally devoted to Santa Maria. Brisk, rational, and somewhat cool in temperament, she regarded her appointment as prima as a duty to be discharged rather than as an opportunity for community recognition or cre-ative input; she was not interested in making major innovations in the festi-val's scheme. A careful, methodical planner with an iron sense of responsibility, she dutifully began planning for the festa about two months in advance. While most primas rely on the telephone or word of mouth to communicate meeting times to the rest of the komitatu, Elena affixed typewritten notes on the obrieres' doors informing them of the time and location of the first meeting—a move immediately criticized as too formal by her political opponents on the komitatu.

Elena's cool rationality found its complementary opposite in Caterina Manzella. Warm, effusive, and an enthusiastic devotee of Santa Maria, Caterina, a 39-year-old nurse, had her own ideas of how the festa ought to be organized, which she never hesitated to express in the clearest of terms. This was apparent from the second meeting, when Caterina announced that the new square at Santa Maria, which was still under construction, was "disgusting." This brought a flurry of complaints from the other committee members about various aspects of the new construction: the square was too small for dancing the ballo tondo; the steps leading to the church were too wide or too steep; the sand which the construction workers had brought in was messy and would get into everyone's shoes on the day of the festa.

Elena did her best to field complaints and bring the discussion back to the actual planning of the festa, but the theme of the church square continued to dominate meetings of the komitatu for Santa Maria during the entire summer of 1986. The criticism was clearly intended as an attack on Elena and the other administrators on the town council for their alleged ineptness at planning and carrying out public works. It was too late in the construction phase of the project for Caterina and her supporters to actually influence the design of the square; in any case, the town council had held an open meeting to receive community suggestions for the square's design the previous spring, and nobody had attended. Rather, it was the first of several attempts Caterina made during the course of planning the festival to challenge Elena's authority as prima and, by extension, as vice-mayor. Even minor issues such as the selection of cookies became occasions for protracted discussion and the expression of political rivalry.

Not one instance of conflict in the festival of Santa Maria in 1986 centered around a major change in the festival program, however. Unlike the Assumption, in which the struggle centers around the negotiation of changes in the festival program, the purpose of most of the arguments between Caterina and Elena (and their respective supporters) was obviously political. What was at stake was power: ritual power within the komitatu as well as political power within the community. The festival became an arena for the enactment of this conflict. The conflict never became a pitched battle because in a number of instances concerning the organization of the festival, Elena let Caterina have her way. Caterina decided on the types and amounts of wine, beer, soda, juice, cookies, and breads; the choice and arrangement of flowers for the church; the washing and ironing of the altar cloths; even the selection of most of the komitatu for the following year were left up to Caterina, the result being that the 1987 committee was loaded with Caterina's political allies. Elena did not object, in part because she genuinely did not care about these details and was happy to leave their decision to someone else, and in part out of a wish to be fair and conciliatory towards a political rival. But her low profile in the festival may also have been a kind of strategy to minimize conflict by dividing ritual and political power between herself and Caterina: Caterina could have all the ritual power connected with Santa Maria and the festival, as long as Elena's political power in the community was not challenged too much.

In part because of this strategy of conflict avoidance, the komitatu did not split into warring factions and the festa of Santa Maria itself never came under direct attack. The community was pleased overall with the results; there were no comments about "deluded obrieri" as there had been for the Assumption. But politically Elena's strategy was not successful; the focus of the community's dissatisfaction became the design and construction of the square. The target of the complaints was Elena herself and the rest of the town council in their official political capacity. It is against this backdrop that Marta Pinna's restoration of the statue of Santa Maria, and her subsequent election as mayor, must be understood.

⚜

Festas, Politics, and Power

David Kertzer (1988) has articulated the importance of public ritual in political life. In describing presidential campaigns in the United States, he states:

> The population is supposed to get to "know" the candidate through his highly ritualized appearances, while the candidate uses the rites to present a certain image of himself and to contrast this with the image he creates of his competitors. (108)

While the festa of Santa Maria occurred several months prior to the election campaigns, a similar principle can be seen to be operating in Marta's management and organization of the festa in 1987. A longtime political activist and member of the D.C., Marta was appointed prima by Caterina Manzella. By spearheading the effort to restore and reconsecrate the antique statue, Marta may have been commenting symbolically on Elena and the P.S.I.'s ineffectiveness in their design and construction of the square, in contrast to her own abilities to give to the community. Her actions were particularly significant and successful because of Santa Maria's importance as a symbol of local identity. Both the Madonna and the festa are perceived as being unique to Monteruju, and numerous elements in the festival work to underline the theme of community solidarity. Because the Assumption has become the locus of dissatisfaction and conflicts following social transformation, the importance of Santa Maria as an occasion for apparent unity and communion has grown. It is one of the few symbols which all Monteruvians value and share. As Kertzer suggests, during times of conflict, shared symbols may be especially important in deflecting social tensions, and "[u]nder the right circumstances, . . . can take on a much more systematic and self-conscious role in bringing about political change" (Kertzer, 1988:150).

Marta and her allies maintain there is no relationship between their successful management of the restoration of Santa Maria and their election to office. When I interviewed her in 1989, Marta claimed that she had never expected to become mayor when she was appointed prima in 1987. "That is a rumor that is being circulated by the opposition to discredit me," she said. "Many people interpret anything that way now; for example, when Antonio and some other boys helped to carry the statue of the Assunta in procession, [people] said it was in order to put themselves on display, when actually it was for devotion." At the same time, Marta is exquisitely sensitive to issues of local pride and to cultural productions as a way of valorizing that sentiment. Since her election, she has organized a number of celebrations and inaugurations, including the rededication of the community center in honor of a young boy tragically killed in a fire.

Each celebration uses and displays local products such as cheeses, cured raw hams, and olives—"to demonstrate how good these genuine, local products are." Like the restoration of the statue, these cultural productions are being manipulated for the creation of a more positive identity for Monteruju. Local foodways become a symbol of authenticity and purity in a larger cultural dialogue that juxtaposes the "traditional" paradigm with the "modern," the rural with the urban, the pastoral with the industrial (cf. Saunders, 1984). The respective attitudes of the D.C. and the P.S.I. can also be made to fit this scheme, with the P.S.I.'s call for progress pushing the community towards a more urban and national culture, while the D.C. in this case offers the means of resistance by valuing the local, the religious, and the traditional. Since numerous dignitaries and politicians were invited to Marta's public celebrations, it seems absurd to argue that festivals and analogous cultural productions have no relationship to politics. The question remains exactly how to characterize that relationship.

It is unlikely that Marta's victory in 1988 was due entirely to her activities on the komitatu the previous year. Many other factors played an important role, including the P.S.I.'s lack of an aggressive pre-election campaign, the growing unemployment rate, a perception that the administration was not doing enough to provide local jobs, and the efforts of outside forces to down Monteruju's socialist majority. Yet within that window of opportunity, Marta was able to draw community attention and approbation by organizing a successful festa that valorized an important local symbol. She was also able to mobilize other members of the komitatu to run for political office on the D.C. ticket, targeting members of families that had previously supported the P.S.I. As a result of this strategy, families that had represented powerful voting blocs were split; individuals voted for their relatives regardless of political denomination, giving a majority of votes to the D.C.

By giving Monteruju a successful festival, Marta demonstrated her abilities to function in the patronal role within the ritual power structure. She was successful because many Monteruvians perceive ritual power and political power to operate in similar ways, according to a *do ut des* paradigm. As Leonardo Piras innocently suggested, the "election" of the Assunta to patronal sainthood following a miracle is not so different from the election of an individual to political office following a good deed or favor to the community. By bringing about the restoration of the antique statue, Marta put herself in a position in which she could receive broad public support. This support served her well several months later during the election campaign, when she could prove that she was capable of acting effectively with the good of the community in mind.

Carnivalesque festivals have long been used as a forum to comment on political or social realities. In this instance, Santa Maria di Runaghes, while not normally a locus of carnivalesque inversion, became a proving ground for power roles that challenged the dominance of the socialist administration. Within the "play" frame of the festa, Caterina, Marta, and their supporters were able to try out new roles that offered an alternative to the existing political reality. Because this form of inversion occurred within the frame of festival, few took it as a serious challenge.

Perhaps it is because of the ludic nature of festivals that few Monteruvians perceive a direct link between ritual power on festival committees and politics. On this issue, the mayor and minority leader were in full agreement. "If anything," Lorenzo Cherchi, the P.S.I. leader and ex-mayor, told me, "festivals exist as a meeting point for people, a place differences can be set aside." "But you were appointed obriere maggiore at Mesaustu the year after you were elected mayor," I argued. "That was a coincidence," he explained. Even Leonardo Piras, who had first drawn my attention to the parallel between ritual and political power, disputed any association between the two. "People say that now because of what has happened," he said, "but there is no relationship between festas and politics." Others were less sure. "I can tell you for a fact that certain individuals would not have been on the council had they not been on the komitatu," Elena asserted. And gossip accusing members of the komitatu of "putting themselves on display" circulated freely in the summer of 1989. What seems clear is that those who had the most to lose through the deconstruction of their actions were the most reluctant to admit any connection between festivals and politics. Those who had little personal stake in either festas or the political situation felt freer to expound on the connections, even in cases when perhaps they were marginal or nonexistent.

While my interpretation is based on a unique set of circumstances, and it is not shared by the majority of Monteruvians, I nevertheless feel a parallel (if not a direct link) exists between ritual and political power. Power of whatever sort, and the relationship between those in power (whether human or sacred) and those beholden to them, is perceived in Monteruju as operating along clientilistic lines. Those who give to the community in the ritual arena are expected to be able to do so in the political sphere, and vice versa. The administrative parallels between a position on the town council and on a komitatu are a further example of the similarity between the two—one that has been expanded by the increasing bureaucratic steps involved in planning and financing a festival. Thus festival committees may also serve as a training ground for those interested in attempting more complex administrative tasks. To be sure, no one serves on a komitatu with the express purpose of obtaining political office. But enough parallels exist between the two positions that under certain circumstances, success on a festival committee can translate into a political victory.

🎗️🎗️

The Politicization of Festival

After the 1988 elections, the two festas took on a decidedly more political cast. Obrieri for the Assunta tend now to be drawn from the P.S.I. and its supporters, while Santa Maria remains in the hands of the D.C. In 1989, for instance, the komitatu for the Assumption included the ex-mayor Lorenzo Cherchi, Elena, and numerous town councilors from their political ranks; the list had been put together by Francesca Manca, herself a town councilor for the P.S.I., whose seat on the council was the object of dispute on the part of the D.C., who would have liked to see it go to one of their representatives. Francesca had good cause to try to prove her capabilities to the townspeople through festival organization. That year, Marta was again appointed prima at Santa Maria, only a year after her election to political office, with the justification that it was the first time in Monteruju's history that an individual could be mayor and prima at the same time. The rivalry continues unabated even during the festival, as each faction competes with the other to show Monteruvians the best possible time.

The conflict played out in the festivals in Monteruju is now predominantly political, but presumably, other conflicts could also come to the fore given a different set of circumstances. For instance, festivals may bring to light the traditional conflict between clergy and laity over the sacred versus the secular role of the festa (Silverman, 1975:165). The priest's attitude towards the komitatu was clearly one of distrust: "These committees take away a bundle of money, all in the name of the Madonna," he said to me. At the same time he lamented the decline in church attendance on festive days and the popularity of the rock and dance bands as the major forms of festive entertainment. On their part, the members of the komitatu try to get around the priest's authority, especially when they wish to introduce a new custom such as decorating the statue of the Madonna with rings or holding the mass outdoors. When a problem occurs involving the religious aspect of the celebration, as it did in 1986 at the Assumption when the guest preacher did not show up, the community is quick to blame the priest, citing his alleged laziness and disregard for festivals as evidence of his culpability.

In the same way, festivals may show up class differences. As one informant put it, during the festival "the lawyer danced with the schoolteacher, and . . . the rich laborer's son wouldn't dare to invite the lawyer's daughter [to dance]." It does create an occasion when the entire community gets together, but within this togetherness, distinctions of class are often maintained. During the festa of Santa Maria in 1986, for instance, a group consisting of the mayor, a teacher, and a member of the town council were chatting together when a fourth individual, a shepherd, approached. "What is this, the intellectuals of Monteruju all hanging out together?" he asked jokingly. The group members, visibly uneasy with this designation, protested laughingly and engaged in a brief interaction with the man, who joked back for a time but eventually wandered off, whereupon the other three immediately resumed their previous conversation. In this instance, the three "intellectuals" became uneasy when a member of another social class pointed out that they were limiting their interactions to each other and excluding him, a member of a lower social class. Embarrassed by this revelation, they modified their behavior briefly but eventually resumed the same pattern.

It is the very nature of festival, as an event which brings community members together for a brief time, to underline both conflict and unity as opposing social groups are brought into contact with each other. How well it succeeds in minimizing conflict while maximizing unity is in part a factor of the ability of the festival organizers to create a package that satisfies the exigencies of the various conflicting groups.

🌿🍃

Two Festas, Two Realities

The Assumption and Santa Maria have become politicized to reflect the two predominant groups vying for power in Monteruju today. But this is only the latest of many incarnations of dualities within the culture that the two festivals express. The two Madonnas have always represented opposite poles in Monteruvian culture: agriculture and pastoralism, village and field, secular and sacred, male and female, "modern" and "traditional." The assumption of political meaning is consistent with the frame of symbolic meanings presently embodied by each festival. In this section, I will examine the development of these frames of meaning to arrive at a better understanding of the relationship of conflict to festive expressions.

Economic Dualism: Agriculture and Pastoralism

Early in the twentieth century, when both agriculture and pastoralism were practiced in Monteruju, the two festivals may have served as expressions and enactments of these two opposite poles in the economy. Although little evidence is available before the beginning of the twentieth century, I would hypothesize that the festivals of the Assunta and St. Martin, her co-patron, peaked in Monteruju in the years preceding the Second World War, when the fascist regime was intent on making Sardinia into the breadbasket of the Italian nation and wheat cultivation was at its maximum level. This was a period which most individuals in their fifties and sixties remember in great detail, as it formed a part of their youth. The memories of these individuals, with their emphasis on the glorious festivals of their youth and adolescence, may give the impression that, in comparison to those times, the Feast of the Assumption in Monteruju is now in decline.

The fact is that we know little about the development of this festival as Monteruju's main patronal feast. Its flowering in the first third of the twentieth century may only have been in correspondence to the economic importance of durum wheat. In fact, we know that the intensive wheat cultivation in the area during the fascist period had a number of other repercussions on the festive cycle. This was the time when, for a short period, the kirka for Santa Maria di Runaghes was also based on grain. The early 1920s saw the development of the committee festival of Santa Lucia (May 1) organized by a group of agricultural laborers—again, mostly connected with the cultivation of wheat. I am suggesting here a direct correlation between the economy of a given area, and not only the economic base but also the symbolic composition of its festivals.

This hypothetical connection is made even more palpable by the dramatic decline of the Feast of the Assumption in comparison to its earlier form as the cultivation of wheat decreased in economic importance after World War II, and by the revival of Santa Maria di Runaghes as the new pastoralism began to flourish after the land reforms of the 1960s and 1970s. Santa Maria's connection to the pastoral economy is evident in its timing to coincide with the beginning of the pastoral year cycle and its partial financing through the donations of sheep by shepherds in the community. In many ways, the revived festa of Santa Maria attempts to reinstate the pre-market festive model. The festival reproduces the old economic model of redistribution and festive consumption, using the new (to Monteruju) economic medium of sheep instead of the old one of wheat. Shepherds donate surplus sheep or older animals that are not expected to survive the winter to the community feast, where they are consumed by all the community members. Cheese, the primary product of the economy, is also donated and consumed. While wine, cookies, and other comestibles served are not direct products of Monteruju's economy, they are included because they are perceived as necessary for a successful meal; but they do not form the main part of the meal, which consists of the mutton stew.

In part in an effort to keep costs down, and in part because they are thought to be more "appropriate" to the Madonna di Runaghes, many other products involved in this festival come from within Monteruju and so contribute to and affirm its economy. Thus wild or homegrown flowers are used for decorating the church, because they are considered more in keeping with its rural atmosphere; plates, cups, napkins, and other disposables are acquired locally; and entertainment is provided by a local group. This concentration on local economic resources accomplishes three things: it keeps the cost of the festival reasonable; it reconstructs the same pattern of social and economic exchange which once existed in the Assumption; and it creates an illusion of independence from the outside world, recalling the self-sufficiency of former times and symbolically calling attention to the community's identity. The economic and the symbolic are thus inextricably intertwined.

Gallini (1977:136–137) has called attention to the economic motivators behind the reviving interest in folklore and the production of folkloric or folklorismic forms. She argues that the economic recessions of the 1970s may have motivated people to return to more homemade forms of entertainment in an effort to keep costs to the minimum. But she also stresses that economics is not the only motivator behind folklore revivals; she sees in them also a kind of testament to the failure of the consumer system to deliver the happiness it had promised. "It then becomes important to find alternative models in which economic and cultural choice become interconnected . . ." (Gallini, 1977:137). In the revival of the festa of Santa Maria di Runaghes, we see the combination of these two motivating factors at work.

Given this evidence, we can theorize that any economic change would be followed by a parallel change in the ritual year cycle. Evidence from this community, as well as from other parts of the island, tends to support this contention. While it has generally been supposed that the year cycle of any given community is relatively set and unchanging, tied to both the agro-pastoral year cycle and the religious calendar, my research in Sardinia indicates a slightly different pattern. Villages customarily shift the celebration dates of their patronal festivals to times that coincide with important economic shifts: for example, Bonorva celebrates its patron saint, Santa Lucia, not on December 13 as in the Catholic calendar, but on May 1, an important time for the planting of many summer crops other than wheat, and a period otherwise unmarked in the Sardinian year cycle. Oschiri celebrates the same patron saint on September 8, a date whose significance in the pastoral year cycle we have fully documented in this study. In recent times, time shifts have also occurred for the sake of convenience. In 1986, the patronal feast of St. George in Pozzomaggiore was shifted by the organizing committee to the following weekend, to take advantage of an extra vacation day on April 26.

Evidence from Monteruju also suggests that, at least since the end of the nineteenth century, festivals in the year cycle have customarily been more fluid than is generally supposed. The festa of Santa Lucia, celebrated in Monteruju on May 1, was created by a group of agricultural laborers who formed the first committee around 1918. The festival of St. Sebastian, once celebrated January 20 according to the Roman Catholic ritual calendar, was shifted for a period of time to mid-May and since 1986 has again been celebrated in January. And the festival of Santa Maria di Runaghes itself has undergone a number of structural changes since the beginning of the twentieth century. These data suggest that the year cycle itself is not a fixed, unchanging pattern, but rather a vehicle for communication open to manipulations both by local forces and by the larger, dominant culture as a whole.

While this may be more evident in recent years because of the dramatic economic changes most peasant communities have undergone, I suspect it is not
a phenomenon confined to modernization but rather is characteristic of the
folkloric process as reflected in year-cycle customs and festivals. It has simply
not been documented before because folklorists usually assume the year cycle
to be relatively fixed and unchanging in any given community.

Symbolism and Ideology

The shift from a predominantly agricultural to a predominantly pastoral
economy is, of course, not the only economic shift Monteruju has experienced in the last thirty years. Monteruju has moved from a peasant to a post-
peasant type of economic system, highly dependent on the world market and
tightly linked to other towns in the vicinity. As we have already noted, the
impact of these changes on the festive system has been considerable. The
result, however, has not been to make festivals "desemanticized" or meaningless, as some scholars have argued; rather, festivals have acquired new significance in accordance with new needs and the new worldview. Elements which
cannot be adapted to the new context are discarded; new elements are introduced which better correspond to a changed reality or convey messages
important to the community. In all of this, the townspeople themselves are
the arbiters of their own symbolic systems, making choices (usually con-
scious) about what to keep, what to change, and what to discard. This manipulation of tradition is the very heart of the folkloric process. Within their
present symbolic frame, the two Madonnas reflect and perform not only
political and economic conflict and struggle, but also the basic contradictions
inherent in a post-peasant way of life. In this sense, they give voice to the conflicts present in nearly every individual at least on some level.

We have already noted how modernization has created in Monteruvian
culture a twin set of paradigms that are often juxtaposed by Monteruvians
themselves: the "old" or "traditional" versus the "modern." For many years,
Monteruju struggled to attain many of the attributes of a "modern" town:
indoor plumbing, electricity, good roads, and other conveniences. The socialist administration was instrumental in diffusing a progressive ideology that
brought many of these desired services to the town. Progressivism, along
with economic and social changes already outlined, soon had its desired
effect. But almost inevitably, once Monteruju had completed the transition
into the post-peasant world, a nostalgia set in for what had been left behind.

This local trend coincided with a more generalized movement within
Italian culture (first in intellectual circles only, then spreading into mass culture) to reevaluate peasant culture. It was not the peasant economy or social
structure that captured the popular imagination, but, in the traditional
romantic frame of Herder and the brothers Grimm, the products of folk culture, including festivals. As Gallini (1977:134) has noted, "The revival of
folklore . . . goes hand in hand with the solemnization of the death of the

peasant world. . . . What become ritualized are only those folkloric forms which can be channeled into the ludic, spectacular or festive spheres, or at any rate into the consumer economy."

In Marxist circles, folk culture was idealized as a source of "alternative culture" in opposition to bourgeois capitalistic culture (Gallini, 1977:133). Agents of the mass media intent on selling "folk" products promulgated the new thesis that "folk," peasant, and rural were now fashionable. Because the cultural transformations that Sardinia has undergone are perceived as acculturation to the dominant Italian culture, these displays also serve as symbolic links to an ethnic or regional culture that is thought to be disappearing, or in any case threatened.

In Monteruju, the reevaluation of peasant culture translates into a growing consciousness of local culture and identity. This reevaluation was a major factor in the revival of Santa Maria di Runaghes and was one of the main reasons for the positive treatment of the rural in this festival. But compared to its neighbors, Monteruju is still close to the rural model which until so recently had been denigrated. Monteruvians have chosen Santa Maria as a forum for the discourse validating the rural, the "folk," the pastoral in local culture and identity. It is no accident that they have chosen Santa Maria for this purpose, as the festival has historic associations with the fields, pastoralism, and things opposed to the civilizing influence of the village. In this community-oriented religious festival run by women and modeled on a family feast, the D.C. found a natural arena for the enactment of the more traditional cultural values the party officially espouses.

Even so, it is important to distinguish between the peasant past, the illusion of the past which the festival attempts to recreate for one evening, and the contemporary reality. As spontaneous as they are, the circle dancing, feasting, and singing that characterize the Santa Maria festival are confined to that festival and do not take place at weddings, christenings, work parties, or in the context of other year-cycle customs in which they at one time were found. The festival of Santa Maria is an occasion that has been deliberately used for the revival of these fading traditions.

In contrast, what we find in the Assumption is a kind of discourse centered in the village but directed towards the outside world: tourists, émigrés, neighboring towns. This discourse declares Monteruju's roots in a regional folk culture at the same time declaring its independence from it. The outside face Monteruju presents during the patronal festa is that of the thoroughly modernized town, so modernized that traditional entertainments are purchased for display rather than participated in freely. The kantadores, poetas, local folk costumes, and folk dance performances represent Monteruju's traditional past but exist on a symbolic level; they may be interpreted as a form of symbolic local identity, akin to the symbolic ethnicity of American ethnic groups (Gans, 1979). What I am suggesting here is that the folklorized forms in the Assumption serve as regional markers that connect Monteruju to Sardinian culture in general, and the regional subculture shared by the other visitors in particular. Together they form a complex of regional markers, distinguishing Monteruvians from the dominant Italian culture around them but linking them to their neighbors from nearby towns. The Assumption, then, embodies the local and regional identity of Monteruju vis-á-vis other Sardinian communities. It is not accidental that the P.S.I. has found in this festival a suitable arena for the performance of its secular, progressive ideology.

We have seen so far how the two festivals, the Assumption and Santa Maria di Runaghes, embody contrasting principles or poles of reality that exist in Monteruju: agriculture and pastoralism, outside relations and community relations, secular world and ritual world, male and female. The two Virgins themselves, the personalities attributed to them by the Monteruvians, and their historic and symbolic associations can be similarly placed in this scheme, as illustrated in table 6 below.[1]

The reason for the coexistence of these two festivals should now be clear. As a model of a culture in the process of change, Monteruju has one foot in the pre-industrial past, the other in the age of computers. The same men who practice sheep herding using paleotechnic methods also operate complicated machinery at their factory jobs; the women who wash at the communal washtubs watch *The Bold and the Beautiful* on television; and the children we see riding behind their grandfather on a donkey are learning to use a computer in school. No single festival can express the full range of modalities present in everyday life in this town; they are at once too complex and contradictory. The solution, for Monteruju, at least, has been to symbolically split those realities by devoting to each its own festival. While the Assumption expresses Monteruju's participation in the modern world, Santa Maria di Runaghes confirms its rootedness in the peasant past. Santa Maria in fact makes the continuation of the Assumption possible by providing a forum in which to satisfy exigencies which the Assumption does not meet. It is possible that if Santa Maria had not been revived, the Assumption would have ceased altogether as well, a victim of the increasingly bitter strife between the new world and the old.

It is difficult to make predictions as to the eventual fate of these festivals. Many Monteruvians make dire predictions about the end of all traditional

Table 6
The Assumption and Santa Maria: Symbolic Associations

The Assumption	Santa Maria
agriculture	pastoralism
male	female
married	unmarried
village	fields
secular	sacred
for outsiders	for community
folklorized	participatory
"modern" ideology	"traditional" ideology
P.S.I.	D.C.

customs before long. As long as the present equilibrium between the festas is maintained, however, the festivals could continue to be observed indefinitely. However, the smallest socioeconomic change can be expected to have repercussions in the celebration of the festivals, and it is difficult to predict what the end result might be. Presently Monteruju continues to hold its own against the encroaching urban sprawl; in 1987, it even acquired its own drugstore. Its elementary school, in contrast, risks being closed altogether if its total enrollment falls much below the present twenty pupils. If this should happen, pupils will be bused to school in nearby Thiesi. This change could conceivably deal a strong blow to the town's sense of community and identity, but paradoxically, it could result in even greater efforts to preserve a local identity through the festa of Santa Maria.

In this chapter we have seen how socioeconomic changes are reflected in a community's festivals and in the organization of the year cycle. Important festivals in the year cycle tend to coincide with times of important agricultural/economic activities (a fact noted by van Gennep); the weight given to festivals changes in response to economic change. This leads us to speculate that the year cycle, that immutable ritual sequence which scans time in all peasant cultures, may actually be less stable than has been previously thought. Moreover, the changes festivals exhibit in response to modernization are not merely financial or organizational but also strike at the symbolic core of the festival itself: festivals are continually evolving in response to current conditions. Festive change is brought about by individuals who, acting singly or together as arbiters of their own symbolic systems, initiate meaningful changes to bring the festivals more in concert with the new situation. When gender, generational, class, and political differences divide a community, these groups may engage in a fierce struggle to determine the form and ideology of the festival. Festival may also become a tool in the construction of local identity for political purposes. Far from being a force that unites the community in utopian harmony, festivals often bring social conflicts to the fore, clearly delineating the competing networks and ideologies operating within village society. In the festivals honoring the two Madonnas, cultural contradictions and conflicting worldviews are brought together and enacted for the whole community to experience. This process at once makes palpable and mediates the contradictions inherent in a post-peasant way of life.

Note

[1] A number of anthropologists have commented on the fragmentation of divine images, which allows the attribution of different powers, characteristics, and sacred locales to icons representing one saint while adhering to a monotheistic religious system (Herzfeld, 1984:653–54). This fragmentation of the saint into a number of different icons is widespread throughout Sardinia and the rest of Italy. Monteruvians do not see a contradiction in the fragmentation of the Virgin into l'Assunta and Santa Maria. "[The Madonna] is always the same," Lucia Tanca told me, "but she has presented herself to us in many ways. The Madonna of Fatima appeared to three shepherds; the Madonna of Lourdes appeared to Bernadette." The Assunta and Santa Maria are thus presented as aspects of the Virgin, each with its characteristic associations.

Afterword

Only a few months after I wrote the wistful Preface to the Second Edition of this book, I had the opportunity—the first in nine years—to return to Monteruju. The occasion was the wedding of a close friend and former informant ("Valentina" in this book) in October 2001. I had many mixed feelings about returning after the events that had transpired since my last visit in 1992; I especially feared that my presence in the village would reawaken old political hostilities and would have negative repercussions for my friends and their families. But I felt bound by a promise I had made Valentina, albeit jokingly, years before: that if she ever got married, I'd return to the village to dance at her wedding. So when she called me during the summer of 2001 and announced that she and her long-time boyfriend were finally going to tie the knot, I felt bound to honor my word.

The wedding was scheduled for the end of October, barely six weeks after the terrorist attacks on New York and Washington, D.C. of September 11, 2001. I arrived in Alghero the day before the ceremony, amid the heightened airport security and travel hysteria that followed the attacks. I had arranged for a rental car at the airport, knowing that my friends would be too busy with wedding preparations to have time to fetch me; as the carabinieri dawdled over my entry visa, checking out my passport for what seemed like hours, I nervously wondered whether I would lose my reservation if I showed up too late. At last I was permitted to pass customs. As I strode through the automatic glass doors towards the rental car pick-up area, I saw a small figure waiting patiently outside, grayer and older but still unmistakably ET. She had come to greet me, unasked, although she knew I had my own transportation. I felt a surge of pure joy at seeing her, and at the same time it felt utterly ordinary, as if the painful events of my last visit had never happened at all.

I knew then that I truly was forgiven.

That evening, I joined Valentina, her family, and my old group of girl-friends at her house as they completed the last-minute preparations for the following day's ceremony. Her mother, elderly now, greeted me with great affection. Valentina looked radiant; my friends were a bit heavier, their hair stylishly cut and dyed to cover the creeping gray, but otherwise much as I had remembered them. "I'm happier to see Sabina again than to see Valentina get married," quipped Franca. I felt like the prodigal daughter returning home at last.

But time had not stood still in Monteruju. I found many more signs of globalization's effects than I noted even in the Preface. The most striking change was the increased economic prosperity. While sheepherding and cheese production remain central economic activities, there are, paradoxi-cally, fewer shepherds. Those that remain have somewhat larger herds and have moved towards more modern means of production. Tonino, Valentina's cousin, proudly showed me his new barn with running water, feeding troughs full of commercial feed to supplement forage, and heated lambing pens for ewes and their offspring. Gone are the *therrakos*, the old tenant-shepherds; while young men may apprentice as shepherds to older relatives, this exploit-ative relationship between large landowners and poor tenants, already fading in the 1980s, has disappeared from the economic landscape due to better employment opportunities in industry and service. Gone, too, are the men who worked as day-laborers, harvesting wheat or olives; today, some of those jobs are done by migrant workers from North Africa. Cheap flights from London (such as the one I took) have brought many more international tour-ists to the island, creating more employment opportunities in the service sec-tor. Satellite TV, now ubiquitous, means Monteruvians have access to BBC, CNN, and international programs from all over Europe.

Evidence of prosperity and the influence of new ideas can be seen every-where in Monteruju, as well as in neighboring towns. Sa Sea, the old thresh-ing ground, has expanded so there are now more residents there than in the historic center of the village. The houses in this new neighborhood are large, two-story buildings with central heating, beautiful tiled bathrooms, and kitchens with new appliances and modern conveniences. Those who live there now consider themselves suburbanites and complain that their neigh-bors who continue to keep chickens, pigs, and sheep are ruining the ambi-ance of the neighborhood. All the streets are now paved; there are no more dirt tracks or gravel roads, even in outlying areas like Sa Silva. The town boasts several brand-new play and picnic spots with swings and outdoor sports equipment, barbecue grills, and eating areas. In the old historic dis-trict, many walls are now painted with brightly-colored *murales* (murals), the handiwork of teams of international exchange students who travel through Europe doing volunteer urban renewal projects. The murals depict local envi-ronmental themes, such as the danger of wildfires and the importance of soil conservation and reforestation.

A good index of the new affluence is the condition of the town's animals. In the mid-1980s few people had animals as pets; the concept of "pet" as companion animal was foreign to the peasant worldview of most Monteruvians. Animals were either livestock, and thus useful, or feral, and thus in competition with humans over resources. Livestock was looked upon as an economic asset and received the minimal veterinary care required by law. Shepherds often kept sheep dogs of no particular breed to guard their flocks from theft during the night. The dogs were fed a diet of bran mixed with water, and occasionally a bone or two; they received no veterinary attention, not even rabies vaccinations. Packs of mangy-looking mongrels roamed the hills at night, often preying on sheep; if shepherds caught them, they could be (and often were) killed on sight. Cats fared no better. Thin strays with perpetual eye infections, torn ears, and abscessed fight wounds slunk about the town's alleys, searching for scraps of food. Some families fed one or two of these, but generally cats were expected to fend for themselves by hunting rodents and other pests. I felt sorry for these creatures and missed my own cats, so at night I would sneak out and put down cat kibble I had purchased for them at the supermarket in Sassari. Monteruvians considered me a bit crazy. The concept of spaying and neutering animals to prevent overpopulation was foreign to them; the most common method of pet population control was the drowning of newborn puppies and kittens.

These attitudes have changed considerably in fifteen years. While the problem of feral dogs and cats has not disappeared, today many more families keep animals as pets. These companion animals live at least partly inside the homes of their owners. Dogs wear collars and are confined to yards or tied in front of houses; even some of the cats wear identification. Monteruvian cats now behave as cats in most Western cities; they respond to human attention and do not shrink from contact. Pets receive regular veterinary care, including vaccinations and contraceptive injections. The new grocery store in Sa Sea, run by one of my old gang of girlfriends, is well-stocked with a variety of dry and canned pet foods that move off the shelves with startling rapidity. A few young Monteruvians even own horses and ride them ostentatiously through the village on Sunday afternoons and during festival parades. Horses have never been important in the Monteruvian economy; in the past, they were owned only by the wealthiest class. Oxen were used for plowing and donkeys for transport, as they are far better suited to the steep mountainous terrain. The renewed presence of the horse as a status symbol indicates that many families have reached a level of affluence that allows them to spend discretionary income to maintain an animal used exclusively for sport. In fact, the existence of pets as a cultural category is a general indicator of the availability of discretionary income, and the changing worldview that allows that surplus to be spent on creatures that have no clear economic function.

The population of Monteruju has also been marked by global flows. It has shrunk to about 400 due to the deaths of many elderly residents and the relocation of most young people to nearby cities to pursue educational and

economic opportunities. But some new citizens are also in evidence. There
has been an influx of returning émigrés from Australia, and now it is not
unusual to hear English as well as Sardo and Italian spoken in the streets.
Since the early 1990s, Italy has been a favorite destination of North African
migrants, and some have found their way to Sardinia. Several Moroccan families now rent houses in the older part of town; the men do the day labor that
local peasants once did, and they also travel to work in other towns. A few
shepherds, rejected by my age-mates in favor of middle-class husbands, have
solved their dilemma by finding mail-order brides from Cuba and Santo
Domingo. These women appear to have adapted quickly to life in Monteruju,
learning Sardo and participating in informal social interactions. The children
of North African migrants and Afro-Caribbean mixed marriages differ in
appearance from the other local children but are reportedly well integrated in
school. It remains to be seen how the presence of different ethnicities and
religions (the Moroccans are Muslim; some of the Cuban and Dominican
immigrants practice Afro-Caribbean religions in addition to Catholicism)
will affect village life and politics in the future.

I was also struck by the presence of a number of women of my generation or younger who have separated from their husbands and now live in the
village with their children. I know few details about the causes of these sepa-
rations, but in each case the women have separated, not divorced, and their
families have accepted the situation, supporting them emotionally and in
some cases financially for a time. The presence of these single mothers in the
village has softened attitudes towards my own situation—even Bettina's, as
two of her nieces are now separated. The mother of one of these women com-
miserated with me over my own divorce. She recited the proverb, "Marriage
is a game of cards; you can win, but you can also lose,"[1] indicating that to
some extent, she believes luck or fate to be a factor in a marriage's success.
However, later in the conversation, she added another proverb, "It takes two
to fight,"[2] expressing her opinion that both parties are ultimately responsible
for disagreements.

There are now many new children in the village, enough to forestall the
closing of the local elementary school for at least several more years. The
children born during my field stays in the mid-1980s are teenagers, and very
aware of global fashion as they craft their appearance. The boys sport spiked
hair and multiple piercings in their ears, noses, and eyebrows, while the girls
either look like new-wave hippies in bell-bottom jeans and long hair or wear
a cap-like pageboy haircut and nose studs. They would look at home on any
California high school or university campus. One thing that has not
changed in Monteruju is the importance of fashion and making a *bella figura*
("good impression").

One of my fears upon returning was that my presence would rekindle old
political arguments about my book, *Le Due Marie di Bessude: Festa e Comunità
in Sardegna* (Magliocco, 1995). I needn't have worried. With the passing of
Marta's right-wing administration and the election of a mixed-party town

council last spring, the political atmosphere has shifted considerably. The struggles over representation that followed the book's publication have been forgotten. Few townspeople have actually read it, but most know about its existence. The book has proved especially popular among returning immigrants, who buy it out of nostalgia; it is also featured on the town's Web site as the only book ever written exclusively about Monteruju. The cause of so much discord and pain only seven years ago has now become a source of community pride.

I hesitate to take any credit whatsoever for this development. But it has also caused me to rethink some of the agonizing self-doubt I experienced in the mid-1990s, when I came to believe that the source of my troubles in Monteruju was both my own deficiency as an ethnographer and the exploitative nature of the ethnographic enterprise itself. It seemed to me that while I had gone into the field to lionize Bettina's culture and undo, in some small way, the class exploitation that characterized her relationship with my grandmother, I had ended up repeating the same old patterns of class oppression and domination. Deeply influenced by the postmodern critique of ethnography (see Clifford, 1986; Tyler, 1986; Abu-Lughod, 1991; Behar, 1993), I began to see my work as part of a discourse that has been used historically to separate elites from non-elites, to delineate the boundaries between oppressor and oppressed, to clarify beyond all doubt that those who were objects of study were also objects of domination. I blamed my difficulties in Monteruju on this paradigm, and on my naïve complicity with it: my romanticism was simply another face of power; the ethnographic gaze was no less intrusive because its practitioner was young, foolish, and idealistic.

Now I'm not so sure anymore. Perhaps the events I described in the two prefaces were caused not by the essentially exploitative nature of ethnography, nor by my inexperience and inadequacy as an ethnographer, but by a combination of factors mostly outside my control. The ethnographies we write have their own trajectories, regardless of our own wishes and agendas. To regard ourselves as the cause of either their vilification or their celebration is a bit hubristic. And while we have an obligation to protect our subjects from harm that may come to them as a result of our writings, and to put their interests ahead of our own advancement, we cannot always shield them, or ourselves, from the fallout that follows the publication of our work.

*   *   *

Soon after the wedding ceremony I ran into Luisa Cossu, who had been involved in the revival of Santa Maria di Runaghes, and who now teaches high school in a nearby city. She embraced me, saying that she had worried about me when she heard the news about the terrorist attacks. "By now you're a part of this community," she said. I was deeply moved by her words, although I did not completely believe them; it is clear to me that I remain in many ways an outsider. Although during this visit I sought to reach a degree of closure around my relationship with Monteruju, I realize now that we are never really done with fieldwork—not as long as our relationships with individuals continue. And in that sense, perhaps, Luisa was right.

Notes

[1] Sardo: *Su matrimoniu este unu giogu de cartes; pote anda bene como pote anda male.*
[2] Sardo: *Bi kere duo po brigare.*

Glossary of Sardinian and Italian Terms

Amaretti — macaroons or almond cookies served at Santa Maria di Runaghes festival

Badde — valley; Badde refers to a large valley west of Monteruju

Ballo civile — ballroom dancing, as opposed to the *ballo tondo* (q.v.)

Ballo tondo — circle dance; traditional folk dance performed at festivals

Ballo Sardo — lit. "Sardinian dance"; recent name for the *ballo tondo*

Bidda — town

Carabiniere — policeman; soldier in the Italian police corps

Carella — street

Cicciones — type of pasta eaten for Feast of the Assumption

Comare — the female godparent of one's child; a female with whom one has formalized relations through godparenthood

Compare — the male godparent of one's child; a male with whom one has formalized relations through godparenthood

Comparatico — the institution of formal godparenthood and the obligations it entails

Comune — Italian term for a municipality or township

Contasscia — Sardinian term for oral narrative, comprising a number of genres

Craxtu de Funari — large rock on a ridge southwest of Monteruju; legendary dwelling place of *Sa Rejusta* (q.v.)

Cuffrate — member of religious fraternity

Cusorre — member of religious sorority

Damas, sas — lit. "the ladies," but used in Monteruju to refer to the titled families who once owned property in the town

137

Domus de janas — lit. "homes of the fairies"; prehistoric shaft tombs

Festa — term in both Italian and Sardinian designating any celebration from a festival to a private party. Used in this work to refer to traditional religious festivals.

Festa de sos forestieri — "festa for outsiders"; Monteruvian term for the days during the Feast of the Assumption which feature elaborate displays of folk dancing and other entertainments aimed at tourists

Festa longa — lit. "long festival"; a festival typically held in a country chapel and characterized by a novena

Festa manna — lit. "big festival"; a community's largest patronal festival

Fritella — a sweet made of fried dough, traditionally served at Carnival

Jolzi — Lit. "George"; a stuffed dummy usually ritually sentenced and "killed" at Carnival

Kantadore (pl. *kantadores*) — traditional singer who performs at festivals

Kapidanni — lit. "head of the year"; Sardinian name for September

Kiliru — round basket used in making *cicciones* (q.v.)

Kirka — lit. "search"; refers to door-to-door ritual begging done by the *komitatu* to collect funds for the festivals

Kizadu — tomato sauce with meat chunks; served with *cicciones* for the Feast of the Assumption

Komitatu — committee in charge of the organization of a festival

Korbula — a large, round, coil-type basket in which grain and *cicciones* are dried; also, a quantity equal to 750 cubic inches

Kottsula in tonte — bread with drippings from roast meat; eaten on *sa notte de 'ennaldzu* (q.v.)

Marias, sas — lit. "the Maries"; Monteruvian term for the period in early September, around the time of Santa Maria di Runaghes (September 8)

Mesaustu, Mesaultu — lit. "mid-August"; the Feast of the Assumption

Mulinu — mill; Mulinu refers to a gorge northwest of Monteruju where at one time a mill used to stand

Mutos — traditional form of singing, usually performed at festivals

Muteddos — traditional Sardinian song type, performed at festivals

Nostra Segnora di Runaghes — Our Lady of Runaghes; celebrated in Monteruju on September 8

Notte de bennaldzu — lit. "January night"; the night of December 31

Nughe-bumbas — smoke bombs or firecrackers at one time set off in front of the homes of *obrieri* at the Assumption

Nuraghe — prehistoric dry stone tower common in Sardinia

Obriere, obriera (pl. *obrieri, obriere*) — member of the *komitatu* to organize a festival

Obriere maggiore — the head of the *komitatu*; chief organizer of a festival

Oberaio, oberaia (pl. *oberaios, oberaias*) — member of a *komitatu*

Piseddo (pl. *piseddos*) — child, youngster; also used to designate unmarried children still living at home

Poeta (pl. *poetas*) — oral improvisational poet who performs at festivals

Primu, prima — the head of a *komitatu*; chief organizer of a festival

Promessa — promise of devotion made to a saint in exchange for some favor

Quota — sum of money contributed by each member of a *komitatu* for financing a festival

Runaghe — Monteruvian term for *nuraghe* (q.v.)

Silva, sa — lit. "the wood"; wooded area south of Monteruju

Secunda — the second in charge of the festival of Santa Maria di Runaghes; always a feminine term. The male equivalent does not exist for the Assumption.

Rejusta, sa — legendary witch-like figure who is said to live under the *craxtu de Funari* (q.v.)

Tenore (pl. *tenores*) — member of a group of four singers who perform in a characteristic style, usually at festivals

Select Bibliography

Aarne, Antti. 1981. *The Types of the Folktale.* Stith T.hompson, trans. and ed. Helsinki: Folklore Fellows Communications No. 184.

Abrahams, Roger. 1972. Christmas and Carnival on St. Vincent. *Western Folklore* 31/4, pp. 275–289.

———. 1982. The Language of Festivals: Celebrating the Economy. In *Celebration*, ed. Victor Turner, pp. 161–177. Washington, DC: Smithsonian Institution Press.

Abrahams, Roger and Richard Bauman. 1978. Ranges of Festival Behavior. In *The Reversible World*, ed. Barbara Babcock, pp. 193–208. Ithaca: Cornell University Press.

Abu-Lughod, Lila. 1991. Writing Against Culture. In *Recapturing Anthropology*, ed. Richard G. Fox, pp.137–162. Santa Fe, NM: School of American Research Press.

Aguilera, F. E. 1978. *Santa Eulalia's People: Ritual Structure and Process in an Andalucian Multicommunity.* New York: American Ethnological Society.

Alziator, Francesco. 1963. Tracce di Rituali Pagani nella Tradizione Popolare Sarda. In *Atti del Convegno degli Studi Religiosi Sardi*, Cagliari (Italy), May 1962. Padova: CEDAM.

———. 1978. *Il Folklore Sardo.* Sassari (Italy): Dessi.

Amades, J. 1940. *El Goigs.* Barcelona: Imatgeria popular catalana.

Angioni, Giulio. 1973. *Rapporti di Produzione e Cultura Subalterna: Contadini in Sardegna.* Cagliari (Italy): EDS.

———. 1989. *I pascoli erranti. Antropologia del pastore in Sardegna.* Naples: Liguore.

Angius, Vittorio. 1833–56. Storia di Logudoro. In *Dizionario Geografico, Storico, Statistico, Commerciale degli Stati del Re di Sardegna*, ed. G. Casalis. Bologna: Forni.

Anfossi, Anna. 1968. *Socialità e Organizzazione in Sardegna.* Milano: Angeli.

Appadurai, Arjun. 1990. "Disjuncture and Difference in the Global Economy." *Theory, Culture and Society* 7: 295–309.

Artizzu, F. 1985. *La Sardegna pisana e genovese.* Sassari (Italy): Chiarella.

Assmuth, Laura. 1997. *Women's Work, Women's Worth: Changing Lifecourses in Highland Sardinia.* Helsinki: Transactions of the Finish Anthropological Society.

Atzeni, Paola. 1988. *Il corpo, i gesti, lo stile. Lavori delle donne in Sardegna.* Cagliari (Italy): CUEC Editrice.

Atzori, Mario and Maria Margherita Satta. 1980. *Credenze e Riti Magici in Sardegna.* Sassari (Italy): Chiarella.

Babcock, Barbara. 1978. Introduction. In *The Reversible World*, ed. Barbara Babcock, pp. 13–38. Ithaca: Cornell University Press.

Bakhtin, Mikhail. 1968. *Rabelais and his World.* Cambridge: Cambridge University Press.

Banfield, Edward C. 1958. *The Moral Basis of a Backwards Society.* New York: Free Press.

Batlle, G. B. 1924. *Los Goigs a Catalunya: consideracions sobra son origen, su influencia su la poesia mistica popular.* Barcelona: L'Arxiu.

Bausinger, Herman. 1986 [1966]. Towards a Critique of Folklorism Critique. In *German Volkskunde*, ed. James R. Dow and Hannjost Lixfeld, pp. 113–123. Bloomington: Indiana University Press.

Behar, R. 1993. *Translated Woman: Crossing the Border with Esperanza's Story.* Boston: Beacon Press.

Beinart, W. 1878. *Il Culto di Maria Oggi.* Rome: Edizioni Paoline.

Bellieni, Carlo. 1973. *La Sardegna e i sardi nella civiltà dell'Alto Medioevo.* 2 volumes. Cagliari (Italy): Fossataro.

Bendix, Regina. 1988. Folklorismus: A Threat or a Challenge? *International Folklore Review* 6: 5–50.

Bessude 1950 "Bessude," in *Dizionario enciclopedico dei comuni d'Italia,* Rome: Ente Librario Italiano, Vol. II, 2, p. 589.

Bianco, Carla. 1974. *The Two Rosetos.* Bloomington: Indiana University Press.

———. 1978. Migration and Urbanization of a Traditional Culture: an Italian Experience. In *Folklore in the Modern World*, ed. Richard M. Dorson. Le Hague: Mouton.

———. 1981. Introduction. In *Festa: Antropologia e Semiotica*, ed. C. Bianco and Maurizio del Ninno. Firenze (Italy): Nuova Guaraldi.

Boscolo, Alberto. 1963. Quadro Storico. In *Sardegna. Enciclopedia Tuttitalia*, pp. 29–49. Firenze (Italy): Sansoni.

———. 1978. *La Sardegna bizantina e alto-giudicale.* Sassari (Italy): Chiarella.

Bottiglioni, Gino. 1925. *Vita Sarda.* Reprinted with new introduction by G. Paulis and M. Atzori, 1978. Sassari (Italy): Dessi.

Brandes, Stanley. 1980. *Metaphors of Masculinity: Sex and Status in Andalusian Folklore.* Philadelphia: University of Pennsylvania Press.

———. 1988 *Power and Persuasion. Fiestas and Social Control in Rural Mexico.* Philadelphia: University of Pennsylvania Press.

Bresciani, Antonio. 1850. *Dei Costumi dell'Isola di Sardegna Comparati con gli Antichissimi Popoli.* Naples: Civiltà Cattolica.

Byrne, Moyra. 1982. Antonio Gramsci's Contribution to Italian Folklore Studies. *International Folklore Review* 2: 70–75.

Cardini, G. 1988. *La Cultura Folklorica.* Busto Arsizio: Bramante Editrice.

Carroll, Michael P. 1986. *The Cult of the Virgin Mary: Psychological Origins* Princeton: Princeton University Press.

Carta Raspi, Raimondo. 1971. *Storia della Sardegna.* Milano: Mursia.

Cecaro, A. M., et al. 1989. *Donne e società in Sardegna: eredità e mutamento.* Sassari (Italy): Iniziative Culturali (TAS).

Cetti, Francesco. 1774–1777. *Descrizione della Sardegna.* 3 vols. N.P.

Cirese, Alberti. 1974–75. Folklore Study in Italy: A systematic profile and bibliography. *Journal of the Folklore Institute* 1974–75/1.

———. 1972. *Cultura Hegemonica e Culture Subalterne.* Palermo: Palumbo.

———. 1974 Folklore in Italy: a Historical and Systematic Profile and Bibliography. *Journal of the Folklore Institute* 11: 2–99.

———. 1963. Sardegna: Folklore, Mito e Realtà Storica. In *Sardegna. Enciclopedia Tuttitalia*, pp. 82–90. Firenze (Italy): Sansoni.

Clifford, James. 1986. Introduction: Partial Truths. In *Writing Culture: The Poetics and Politics of Ethnography*, ed. James Clifford and George Marcus, pp. 1–26. Berkeley: University of California Press.

———. 1988. *The Predicament of Culture*. Cambridge: Harvard University Press.

Cocchiara, Giuseppe. 1963. *Il mondo alla rovescia*. Torino (Italy): Boringhieri.

———. 1980 *Il paese di Cuccagna*. Torino (Italy): Boringhieri.

———. 1981. *The History of Folklore in Europe*. Philadelphia: Institute for the Study of Human Issues.

Contini, Giuseppe. 1977. *Codice delle Leggi della Regione Sarda*. Milano: Giuffrè.

Coretti, Paolo. 1982. I Culti Mariani nel Lazio: la Madonna del Parto e la Madonna del Buon Consiglio. Ph.D. thesis, University of Rome.

Costa, Enrico. 1911. *I Costumi Sardi*. Sassari (Italy): Dessi.

———. 1937. *Sassari*. Sassari (Italy): Dessi.

Counihan, Carole M. 1985. Transvestism and Gender in a Sardinian Carnival. *Anthropology* 9, 1–2: 11–24.

Da Re, Maria Gabriella. 1990. *La casa e i campi. Divisione sessuale del lavoro nella Sardegna tradizionale*. Cagliari (Italy): CUEC Editrice.

Davis, Natalie Zeamon. 1978. Women on Top: Symbolic Sexual Inversion and Political Disorder in Early Modern Europe. In *The Reversible* World, ed. Barbara Babcock, pp. 147–190. Ithaca: Cornell University Press.

Dégh, Linda. 1965. Processes of Legend Formation. Separatum. Athens: International Congress for Folk Narrative Research, Athens.

———. 1969. *Folktales and Society*. Bloomington: Indiana University Press.

———. 1972. Folk Narrative. In *Folklore and Folklife*, ed. Richard M. Dorson, pp. 53–84. Chicago: University of Chicago Press.

———. 1983. Kákasd Revisited. In *New Hungarian Peasants*, ed. Marida Hollos and Bela Maday. East European Monograph Series 34. New York: Columbia University Press.

Dégh, Linda and Andrew Vázsonyi. 1976. Legend and Belief. In *Folklore Genres*, ed. Dan Ben-Amos, pp. 93–123. Austin: University of Texas Press.

Delitala, Enrica. 1963. Il Vescovo Pietrificato: Sassari e Logudoro, Usi e Costumi. In *Sardegna. Enciclopedia Tuttitalia*, pp. 294–300. Firenze (Italy): Sansoni.

Del Ninno, Maurizio. 1983. La corsa dei ceri a Gubbio: stato di una ricerca. *Quaderni di antropologia e semiotica*, 1/1: 1–26.

DeRosa, G. 1981. *La Religione Popolare*. Rome: Edizioni Paoline.

Dessany, S. 1946. Origini Bizantine delle Sagre in Sardegna. Almanacco Letterario *Artistico della Sardegna* 1/1: 192–195.

Di Nola, Alfonso. 1972. Religione dei sardi. In *Enciclopedia delle Religioni*, vol. 5, pp. 830–834. Firenze (Italy): Vallecchi.

Dizionario Enciclopedico dei Communi d'Italia. 1950. "Bessude" entry. Rome: Ente Librario Italiano. Vol. II, p. 589.

Dundes, Alan and Alessandro Falassi. 1975. *La Terra in Piazza: an Interpretation of the Palio of Siena*. Berkeley: University of California Press.

Durkheim, Émile. 1915. *The Elementary Forms of the Religious Life*. London: George Allen & Unwin, Ltd. (Reprinted in paperback by Free Press, 1965.)

Enna, Francesco. 1984. *Sos Contos de Foghile*. Sassari (Italy): Edizioni Gallizzi.

Falassi, Alessandro. 1980. Definition and Morphology. In *Time out of Time: Essays on the Festival*, ed. A. Falassi, pp. 1–7. Albuquerque: University of New Mexico Press.

Fél, Edit and Tamas Hofer. 1969. Proper Peasants: Traditional Life in a Hungarian Village. Wenner-Gren Foundation for Anthropological Research 46.

Ferraro, Giuseppe. 1967 [1891]. *Canti Popolari in Dialetto Logudorese*. Bologna: Forni.

———. 1894. Feste Sacre e Profane. *Archivio per lo Studio delle Tradizioni Popolari* 13.

Foster, George. 1967. Peasant Personalities. In *Peasant Society: A Reader*, ed. Potter, Diaz, and G. Foster, pp. 2–13. Berkeley: University of California Press.

Franklin, S. H. 1969. *European Peasantry: The Final Phase*. London: Methuen.

Friedman, Jonathan. 1990. "Being in the World: Globalization and Localization." *Theory, Culture and Society* 7: 311–328.

Fuos, J. 1780. *Nachrichten aus Sardinien von der gegenwürtigen Verfassung dieser Insel*. Leipzig: N.P.

Galanti, Maria Bianca. 1950. Forms and Aspects of the Ballo Tondo Sardo. *Journal of the International Folk Music Council* 2: 14–16.

Gallini, Clara. 1971. *Il Consumo del Sacro: Feste Lunghe di Sardegna*. Bari (Italy): Laterza.

———. 1977. *Tradizioni Sarde e Miti d'Oggi*. Cagliari (Italy): EDS.

Gans, Herbert. 1979. Symbolic Ethnicity: the Future of Ethnic Groups in America. *Ethnic and Racial Studies* 2/1, pp. 1–19.

Geertz, Clifford. 1962. Studies in Peasant Life: Community and Society. In *Biennial Review of Anthropology*, ed. B. Siegel, pp. 1–42. Stanford: Stanford University Press.

———. 1973a. "Deep Play": Notes on the Balinese Cockfight. In *The Interpretation of Cultures*, ed. C. Geertz, pp. 412–454. New York: Basic Books.

———. 1973b. Ritual and Social Change: A Javanese Example. In *The Interpretation of Cultures*, ed. C. Geertz, pp. 142–169. New York: Basic Books.

Glassie, Henry H. 1975. *All Silver and No Brass: An Irish Christmas Mumming*. Bloomington: Indiana University Press.

Gluckman, H. Max. 1963. Rituals of Rebellion in South-East Africa. In *Order and Rebellion in Tribal Africa*, pp. 110–136. London: Cohen & West.

Greenwood, Davydd. 1977. Culture by the Pound: An Anthropological Perspective on Tourism as Cultural Commodization. In *Hosts and Guests: The Anthropology of Tourism*, ed. Valene Smith, pp. 129–138. Philadelphia: University of Pennsylvania Press.

Hager, G. 1902. *Die Weihnachtskrippe*. Munich: Kommissionsverlag der Gesellschaft für christliche Kunst.

Herzfeld, Michael. 1982. *Ours Once More: Folklore, Ideology and the Making of Modern Greece*. Austin: University of Texas Press.

———. 1984. The Significance of the Insignificant: Blasphemy as Ideology. *Man* 19, 653–664.

———. 1987. "As in Your Own House": Hospitality, Ethnography and the Stereotype of Mediterranean Society. In *Honor and Shame and the Unity of the Mediterranean*, ed. David Gilmore, pp. 75–89. Washington, DC: American Anthropological Association.

———. 1987. *Anthropology through the Looking Glass: Critical Ethnography in the Margins of Europe*. Cambridge: Cambridge University Press.

Hobsbawm, Eric and Terence Ranger (eds.). 1983. *The Invention of Tradition*. Cambridge: Cambridge University Press.

Hollos, Marida and Bela C. Maday. 1983. *New Hungarian Peasants.* New York: Columbia University Press Social Science Monographs.

Huizinga, Johan. 1950. *Homo Ludens: A Study of the Play Element in Culture.* Boston: Beacon Press.

Hymes, Dell. 1975. Breakthrough into Performance. In *Folklore: Performance and Communication,* ed. Dan Ben-Amos and Kenneth Goldstein, pp. 11–73. Le Hague: Mouton.

Kertzer, David I. 1988. *Ritual, Politics and Power.* New Haven: Yale University Press.

La Marmora, Alberto. 1826. *Voyage en Sardaigne.* Transl. Italian 1975. Bologna: Forni.

Lanternari, Vittorio. 1963. Dalla Preistoria al Folklore nelle Tradizioni Popolari Sarde. Atti del Convegno degli Studi Religiosi Sardi, Cagliari (Italy), May 1962. Padova: CEDAM.

———. 1981. Spreco, ostentazione, competizione economica: antropologia del comportamento festivo. In *Festa: antroplogia e semiotica,* ed. Carla Bianco and M. del Ninno, pp. 132–150. Firenze (Italy): Nuova Guaraldi.

———. 1984. *Preistoria e Folklore: Tradizioni Etnografiche e Religiose della Sardegna.* Sassari (Italy): L'Asfodelo.

Lawless, Elaine. 1981. Women's Life Stories and Reciprocal Ethnography as Feminist and Emergent. *Journal of Folklore Research* 28/1: 35–60.

LeLannou, Maurice. 1941. *Patres et Paysans de la Sardaigne.* Transl. Italian Manilio Brigaglia, 1979. Cagliari (Italy): La Torre.

Lilliu, Giovanni. 1963. *La civiltà dei sardi dal Neolitico all'età dei nuraghi.* Torino (Italy): ERI.

Lombardi-Satriani, Luigi. 1974. Folklore as Culture of Contestation. *Journal of the Folklore Institute* 11: 99–121.

Lopreato, Joseph. 1967. *Peasants No More.* San Francisco: Chandler.

Lortat-Jacob, B. 1981. Community Music and the Rise of Professionalism: A Sardinian Example. *Ethnomusicology: Journal of the Society for Ethnomusicology* 25/2 (1981): 185–197.

Luciano, Baldassarre. 1841. *Cenni sulla Sardegna,* 2nd ed. Torino (Italy): Botta.

Mannhardt, Wilhelm. 1875. *Der Baumkultus der Germanen und ihrer nachbarstämme.* Berlin: Gebrüder Borntraeger.

MacCannell, Dean. 1976. *The Tourist.* New York: Schocken Books.

Magliocco, Sabina. 1995. *Le due Marie di Bessude: festa e trasformazione sociale in Sardegna.* Ozieri (Italy): Il Torchietto.

———. 2001. Coordinates of Power and Performance: Festivals as Sites of (Re)Presentation in Sardinia. *Ethnologies* 23/1: 167–188.

Manning, Frank. 1983. Introduction. In *The Celebration of Society,* ed. Frank Manning. Bowling Green, OH: Bowling Green University Press.

Marcus, George and Michael Fischer. 1986. *Anthropology as Cultural Critique.* Chicago: University of Chicago Press.

Mathias, Elizabeth. 1974. *From Folklore to Mass Culture: The Dynamics of Acculturation in the Games of Italian-American Men.* Ph.D. Dissertation, University of Pennsylvania.

McDonald, Maryon. 1989. *"We Are Not French!" Language, Culture and Identity in Brittany.* London: Routledge.

Meloni, Benedetto. 1984. *Famiglie di Pastori: Comunità e Mutamento in una Comunità della Sardegna Centrale,* 1950–1970. Torino (Italy): Rosenberg and Seller.

Meloni, P. 1975. *La Sardegna romana.* Sassari (Italy): Chiarella.

Mesnil, Marianne. 1987. Place and Time in Carnivalesque Festival. In *Time Out of Time: Essays on Festival,* ed. A. Falassi, pp. 184–196. Albuquerque: University of New Mexico Press.

Moretti, P. 1958. *Poesia popolare Sarda.* Firenze (Italy): Olschki.

Moser, Hans. 1962. Vom Folklorismus in unserer Zeit. *Zeitschrift für Volkskunde* 58: 177–209.

———. 1964. Der Folklorismus als Forschungsproblem der Volkskunde. *Hessische Blätter für Volkskunde* 55: 9–57.

Murru Corriga, G. 1977. Ethia, lingua, cultura: un dibattito aperto in Sardegna. Cagliari: Edes.

Musumarra, G. 1957. *La sacra rappresentazione della natività nella tradizione italiana.* Firenze (Italy): L. S. Olschki.

Narayan, Kirin. 1989. *Storytellers, Saints and Scoundrels.* Philadelphia: University of Pennsylvania Press.

Odermatt, Peter. 1996. A Case of Neglect? The Politics of (Re)Presentation: A Sardinian Case. In *Coping with Tourists: European Reactions to Mass Tourism,* ed. Jeremy Boissevain, pp. 84–111. Providence: Berghahn Books.

Oppo, Anna, ed. 1990. *Famiglia e matrimonio nella società sarda tradizionale.* Cagliari (Italy): La Tarantola.

Palmas, Gavino. 1974. *Thiesi: Villa Antifeudale.* Cagliari (Italy): Fossataro.

Paulis, Giulio. 1983. *Lingua e Cultura nella Sardegna Bizantina.* Sassari (Italy): L'Asfodelo.

Pettazzoni, Raffaele. 1912. *La Religione Primitiva in Sardegna.* Piacenza (Italy): Società Editrice Pontemolese.

Pillonca, Paolo. 1982. La Poesia Improvisata. In *Enciclopedia La Sardegna,* ed. Manilio Brigaglia and A. Mattone, pp. 149–155. Cagliari (Italy): Della Torre.

Pinna, Luca. 1971. *La Famiglia Esclusiva: Parentela e Clientilismo in Sardegna.* Bari (Italy): Laterza.

Pira, Michelangelo. 1968. *Sardegna tra due lingue.* Cagliari (Italy): La Zattera.

———. 1978. *La rivolta dell'oggetto. Antropologia della Sardegna.* Milano: Giuffrè.

Piras, Gabriele. 1961. *Storia del Culto Mariano in Sardegna.* Cagliari: Scuola Tipografica Francescana.

Pitkin, Donanld S. 1954. Land Tenure and Family Organization in an Italian Village. Harvard University Ph.D. dissertation.

Pitt-Rivers, Julian. 1971 [1954]. *People of the Sierra.* Chicago: University of Chicago Press.

Pittau, Massimo. 1970. Lingua e civiltà in Sardegna. Cagliari: Editrice Sarda Fossataro.

Redfield, Robert. 1956. *Peasant Society and Culture.* Chicago: University of Chicago Press.

Rosaldo, Renato. 1989. *Culture and Truth.* Boston: Beacon Press.

Ruby, Jay (ed.). 1982. *A Crack in the Mirror: Reflexive Perspectives in Anthropology.* Philadelphia: University of Pennsylvania Press.

Sanna, Salvatorica. 1969. Contributo al Repertorio e all'Atlante Demologico Sardo: Inchiesta nel Meilogu. Ph.D. thesis, University of Cagliari.

Satta, Maria Margherita Gabriella. 1980. *Donne e Preghiere Tradizionali in Sardegna.* Quaderni Demologici 3. Sassari (Italy): L'Asfodelo.

———. 1982a. La Religiosità e le Feste. In *La Sardegna,* ed. Mario Brigaglia, pp. 125–139. Cagliari (Italy): Della Torre.

———. 1982b. *Riso e Pianto nella Cultura Popolare: Feste e Tradizioni Sarde.* Sassari (Italy): L'Asfodelo.

Saunders, George R. 1981. Men and women in Southern Europe. *Journal of Psychoanalytic Anthropology* 4/4: 435–466.

———. 1984. Contemporary Italian Cultural Anthropology. *Annual Review of Anthropology* 13: 447–466.

Silverman, Sydel. 1975. *The Three Bells of Civilization: The Life of an Italian Hill Town*. New York: Columbia University Press.

Smith, Robert J. 1975. *The Art of the Festival*. Lawrence: University of Kansas Publications in Anthropology 6.

Smith, Waldemar R. 1977. *The Fiesta System and Economic Change*. New York: Columbia University Press.

Smyth, Sir William Henry. 1828. *Sketch of the Present State of the Island of Sardinia*. London: John Murray.

Sole, Carlino. 1982. Storia dell'Agricoltura. In *La Sardegna*, ed. Mario Brigaglia and A. Mattone, pp. 5–16. Cagliari (Italy): Della Torre.

Stallybrass, Peter and Allon White. 1986. *The Politics and Poetics of Transgression*. Ithaca: Cornell University Press.

Stefanucci, A. 1944. *Storia del Presepio*. Rome: Autocultura.

Stoeltje, Beverly J. 1983. Festival in America. In *Handbook of American Folklore*, ed. Richard M. Dorson, pp. 239–246. Bloomington: Indiana University Press.

———. 1989. Festival. In *Encyclopedia of Communication*, ed. Erik Barnouw. New York: Oxford University Press.

Tedeschi, Florenza. 1980. Asta e Questua nel Rapporto fra Organizzazione Cerimoniale e Organizzazione del Lavoro. Ph.D. thesis, University of Florence.

Thompson, Stith. 1955–58. *Motif Index of Folk Literature*, rev. ed. Copenhagen and Bloomington: Indiana University Press.

Tola, Emanuele. 1983. *Un Illustre Casato Sardo: Marongio, Note Genealogiche e Biografiche*. Sassari (Italy): Chiarella.

Toschi, Paolo. 1969. *Le origini del teatro italiano*. Torino (Italy): Boringhieri.

Tradizioni Orali non Cantate. 1975. Tradizioni orali non cantate. Primo inventario nazionale per tipi, motivi o argomanti di fiabe, leggende, storie e aneddoti.... di cui alle registrazioni sul campo promosse dalla Discoteca di Stato in tutte le regioni italiane negli anni 1968–69 e 1972, ed. Alberto Cirese and Liliana Serafini. Rome: Ministero dei beni culturali e ambientali.

Turner, Victor. 1969. *The Ritual Process: Structure and Anti-Structure*. Ithaca: Cornell University Press.

———. 1974. *Dramas, Fields and Metaphors: Symbolic Action in Human Society*. Ithaca: Cornell University Press.

———. 1978. Comments and Conclusions. In *The Reversible World*, ed. Barbara Babcock, pp. 276–296. Ithaca: Cornell University Press.

———. 1983. The Spirit of Celebration. In *The Celebration of Society*, ed. Frank Manning. Bowling Green, OH: Bowling Green University Press.

Turner, Victor and Edith Turner. 1978. *Image and Pilgrimage in Christian Culture*. New York: Columbia University Press.

Tyler, Stephen A. 1986. Post-Modern Ethnography: From Document of the Occult to Occult Document. In *Writing Culture: The Poetics and Politics of Ethnography*, ed. James Clifford and George Marcus, pp. 122–140. Berkeley: University of California Press.

van Gennep, Arnold. 1909. *Les Rites de Passage*. Paris: Emile Nourry.

———. 1951. *Manuel de Folklore Francais Contemporain*. Paris: Editions Picard.

Wagner, Max Leoppold. 1951. *La Lingua Sarda*. Berne (Italy): A. Francke.

———. 1960. *Dizionario Etimologico Sardo*. Heidelberg: Carl Winter, Universitätsverlag.

Weingrod, Alan and E. Morin. 1973. Post-Peasants: The Character of Contemporary Sardinian Society. *Comparative Studies in Sociology and History* 13/2: 301–324.

Weber-Kellerman, I. 1963. "Volkskundliche Betrachtungen zum ländlichen Gross-betrieb im 19. Jahrhundert. (Im Zusammenhang mit dem Mannhardt-Fragebo-gen von 1865)," *Marburger Universitätsbund Jahrbuch*, pp. 501–529.

———. 1965. "Erntebrauch in der ländlichen Arbeitswelt des 19. Jahrhunderts. Auf Grund der Mannhardtbefragung in Deutschland von 1865." *Volksforchung an der Philipps-Universität Marburg*, Lahn. A, vol. 2.

Weiser, Francis X. 1958. *Handbook of Christian Feasts and Customs*. New York: Harcourt, Brace & World.

Wolf, Eric. 1966. *Peasants*. Foundations of Modern Anthropology Series. New York: Prentice-Hall.

Wylie, Lawrence. 1974. *Village in the Vaucluse*. Cambridge, MA: Harvard University Press.

Index

Bib. # 533 633

394. 269459
MAG

Ollscoil na hÉireann, Gaillimh

3 1111 40231 7802